S U S T A I N A B L E

P E A C E

Angola's Recovery

With best regards

D

New York
7 April 93

Compiled
by
David Sogge

SARDC

Southern African Research and Documentation Centre
Box 5690, Harare, Zimbabwe
1992

SARDC
Southern African Research and Documentation Centre
Box 5690, Harare, Zimbabwe

© SARDC 1992

Cover Design By Rebecca Garret

ISBN 0-7974-1113-5

Printed by Jongwe Printing & Publishing Company (Pvt) Ltd
14 Austin Road, Harare, Zimbabwe

Desktop Publishing by Vijay Thadani, ACCESS Computer Services
Private Bag 8447, Causeway, Harare, Zimbabwe

CABINDA

Chicamba
Belize
Cagongo
Cabinda

ZAIRE

ZAIRE

N'zeto

Luvo
M'banza Kongo
Tomboco
Songo
Uige
UIGE
Negage

Maquela do Zombo
Quimbele
Massango

Chitato
Andrada
Cambulo

Canacassala
Kifangondo
Caxito
Quibaxe
LUANDA
LUANDA
CUANZA NORTE
N'dalatando
Cabala
BENGO
Cambambe
Dondo
Pungo Andongo
CAMBABE DAM
Quitembo
MALANJE
Malanje

Luremo
Cuango

Lucapa
LUNDA NORTE
Saurimo

Cacolo
LUNDA SUL
Muconda

Mussende
Quibala
CUANZA SUL
Gabela

Waku Kungo
HUAMBO
Luimbala
Alto Hama
Katchiungo
Huambo
Cuima
Gove

N'harea
Andulo
Kuito
Camacupa
BIE

Cazaga
Luena
Luacano
Cazombo

Luau
Caianda

MOXICO
Lucusse

ATLANTIC OCEAN

Lobito
Benguela
Alto
Catumbela
BENGUELA

Lucira
Bibala
Lubango
Capelongo
Chiange
NAMIBE
Namibe
Tombwa
Foz do Cunene

Coconda
Caluquemba
Quilengues
HUILA
Matala
Cassinga
Kuvango

Menongue

Lumbala N'Guimbo

Ninda

ZAMBIA

Cuito Cuanavala
Caiundo
KUANDO KUBANGO
Mavinga

Xangongo
CUNENE
Ngiva

Mucusso
Luiana
Jamba

NAMIBIA

ZAIRE

Donors

The Southern African Research and Documentation Centre (SARDC) wishes to acknowledge with thanks the support given for the research, publication, translation and distribution of this book by the following organizations:

Swedish International Development Authority (SIDA)

Canadian International Development Agency (CIDA)

Mission Française de Coopération et d'Action Culturelle

United Nations Children's Fund (UNICEF)

AWEPAA/African European Institute

Contents

List of Tables

List of Figures

List of Photographs

Acknowledgements

This book would not have been possible without the collective efforts of many people who provided ideas, contacts, suggestions, and guidance. Dozens of Angolans from all walks of life contributed immensely, for it is truly a book about Angolans, by Angolans.

Others contributed their special knowledge about, and commitment to, Angola. Many worked under extremely trying and difficult circumstances to bring new and up-to-date information to readers. The compiler, donors and publishers gratefully acknowledge the help offered by the following persons who assisted in gathering the material:

Samuel Aco, Arlindo Barbeitos, Paulo Barcia, Lothar Berger, Stefaan van den Borght, Vergílio Coelho, Allan Cain, Henrique Chitas, Andrew Couldridge, Dag Ehrenpreis, Ibrahima Doc Fall, Phyllis Johnson, Birgitta Lagerstrom, Carlos Machado, Mário Nelson Maximino, Hugh McCullum, Bill Minter, Françoise Mompoint, Júlio de Morais, Ana Maria de Oliveira, Fernando Pacheco, Marli Pinto, Carl-Johan Regnell, Paul Robson, Charles Rubayiza, Gina Sapalalo, Vítor Serrano, Bernard Sexe, Paul Staal, Finn Tarp, Luandino Viera, Fernanda Vítor, Julia Williamson, Bob van der Winden and Henk van Zuidam.

Without the writers, co-ordinators, researchers and journalists in Angola who laboured to meet deadlines under strenuous circumstances the information on the ground would still be there, instead of between the covers of this book.

Key to all this was Maria Lectícia Saraiva Pereira de Almeida e Silva, who was the General Coordinator for the book in Angola. Mary Guinapo was the administrative coordinator in Luanda.

José (Jonuel) Goncalves, economist-journalist, member of the Executive Committee of CODESRIA, was a key writer and advisor to the project.

Others from Angola who played an integral role and whose material appears throughout were: José Ribeiro, senior journalist; and Marina de Almeida, Márcia Coelho, Ilda Carreira, Sara Fialho, Alvaro Macieira and Antonio Kiala Pindi.

Foreign journalists with experience in Angola who contributed important sections were Loes van den Bergh, Vicki R. Finkel and Susan Hurlich.

People gave unstintingly of their time and knowledge, far more than can be acknowledged here. For anyone who has been left out, my apologies, and at the same time my assurance that their help was invaluable.

Special thanks are due to Phyllis Johnson and Hugh McCullum of the Southern African Research and Documentation Centre (SARDC) for their careful reading and editing of the manuscript in its many drafts. The desktop publishing of Vijay Thadani and the cover design by Rebecca Garrett add immeasurably to the final product. Memory Sachikonye and Akin Adegbola assisted greatly in co-ordinating the production of the final manuscript.

Without the support of the Swedish International Development Authority (SIDA), the Canadian International Development Agency (CIDA), the United Nations Children's Fund (UNICEF), and Mission Française de Coopération et d'Action Culturelle de l'Ambassade de France, Luanda and AWEPAA/African European Institute, the book would not have been possible. For their financial resources, accommodation, travel assistance and overall help including distribution of this book, the compiler, publishers and organizers of this project are most grateful.

Finally, for any factual errors or omissions which may have inadvertently occurred, I take full responsibility. My thanks to everyone connected to this book.

David Sogge
Harare, Zimbabwe
July, 1992.

Glossary

AA   Acção Angolana para o Desenvolvimento (Angolan Action for Development), an Angolan NGO.

ACA   Associação Cívica Angolana (Angolan Civic Association), an Angolan pressure group.

ADRA   Acção para o Desenvolvimento Rural e Ambiente (Action for Rural Development and the Environment), an Angolan NGO.

AEA   Associação dos Evangélicos de Angola (Association of Evangelicals of Angola).

ANGOP   Agencia Angola Press (Angolan Press Agency).

Assimilados Africans and *mestiços* whom the Portuguese state considered to have mastered the Portuguese culture and language, and were, therefore, eligible for Portuguese citizenship.

Bakongo   Ethnic group (language: *Kikongo*) of northwestern Angola; estimated by the Portuguese to constitute about 14 percent of the Angolan African population in 1960.

CAIE   Conselho de Igrejas Evangélicas de Angola (Angolan Council of Protestant Churches).

Caritas   Angolan NGO, the charitable branch of the Roman Catholic Church in Angola.

CCPM   Comissão Conjunta Politico-Militar (Joint Political-Military Commission, JPMC).

CONGA   Comité de Organizações Não-Governamentais em Angola (Committee of Non-Governmental Organizations in Angola).

DNSP   Direcção Nacional de Saúde Pública (National Directorate of Public Health).

FLEC   Frente de Libertação do Enclave de Cabinda (Cabinda Enclave Liberation Front).

FONGA   Fórum das ONGs Angolanas (Forum of Angolan Non-Governmental Organizations).

FNLA   Frente Nacional de Libertação de Angola (National Front for the Liberation of Angola).

GDP   Gross Domestic Product (In Portuguese = PIB, Produto Interno Bruto).

ILO   International Labour Organization (Organização Internacional de Trabalho, OIT).

INE   Instituto Nacional de Estatística (National Institute of Statistics).

Kz   Kwanza. National currency of Angola, renamed the New Kwanza (NKw) in September 1990.

Mestiços	People of mixed race.
MPLA	Movimento Popular de Libertação de Angola (Popular Movement for the Liberation of Angola). From 1977 to 1991 its official designation was MPLA-Partido do Trabalho or MPLA-PT, MPLA-Workers' Party.
MUSA	Movimento para a Unidade Socialista em Angola (Movement for Socialist Unity in Angola).
NGO	Non-governmental organization.
OMA	Organização da Mulher Angolana (Organization of Angolan Women).
Ovimbundu	Ethnic group (language: *Umbundu*) occupying chiefly the provinces of Benguela, Huambo and Bie (including the "central highlands"); estimated by the Portuguese to constitute about 38 percent of the African population in 1960.
PAG	Programa de Acção do Governo (Action Programme of the Government).
Patrões	bosses, owners; plural of *patrão*.
PIDE	Polícia Internacional para a Defesa do Estado (International Police for the Defence of the State), the Portuguese secret police under Salazar; acronym later changed to DGS.
SEAS	Secretariado do Estado de Assuntos Sociais (State Secretariat of Social Affairs).
SEF	Saneamento Económico e Financeiro (Economic and Financial Restructuring).
Soba	African figure of traditional authority, chief.
SWAPO	South West Africa People's Organization.
Tocoístas	Adherents of the Church of Our Lord Jesus Christ on Earth (Igreja de Nosso Senhor Jesus Cristo no Mundo).
UEA	União dos Escritores Angolanos (Angolan Writers' Union).
Umbundu	Ethnic group (language: *Kimbundu*) inhabiting chiefly the area from Luanda to the eastern edge of Malanje province; estimated by the Portuguese to constitute about 23 percent of the African population in 1960.
UNACA	União Nacional dos Camponeses Angolanos (National Union of Angolan Peasants).
UNDP	United Nations Development Programme (Programa das Nações Unidas para o Desenvolvimento, PNUD).
UNICEF	United Nations Children's Fund.
UNITA	União Nacional para a Independencia Total de Angola (National Union for the Total Independence of Angola).
UNTA	União Nacional dos Trabalhadores Angolanos (National Union of Angolan Workers).

Historical Note

"The history of the modern conquest of Angola is irrigated by blood of the victims."[1]

The burden of Angola's past is heavy, like the shackles of the slave-gangs. Aggression and resistance have marked its history from the earliest days of contact with Europe.

Behind that history has been the promise of gain, even of riches, for Angolan and foreigner alike. "Any history of Angola, then, that makes sense, must be an economic history."[2]

Trade and the drive to control labour, to possess the land and exploit what lay beneath it has motivated those with political interest, who in turn have been the ones to hire, equip and direct those with the weapons.

"In reality, if the inhabitants of Angola have fought more frequently than other Africans, it was not because they had suffered uncommon blows in the history of colonization in tropical areas. It was because they faced adversaries who combined material debility with excessive greed."[3]

Aggression and avarice have shaped Angola's life as a nation down to the present day. Some facts and dates, reviewed here briefly, suggest how often they recurred. Indeed, they provide the main counterpoints to the themes of this book.

The following historical chronology provides an overview of Angola's past. Major political and military events between 1974 and 1992 are given special attention because they form references for the trends discussed in the book's main chapters.

1483	First Portuguese arrive, beginning contact with the Kongo Kingdom, whose king was an elected official. Shortly thereafter, "*cooperantes*" arrive, attempts at Christianization begin, and export of slaves and ivory starts.
1530	Slave export now at 5,000 a year. Over the next 300 years, some 4 million Angolans were shipped overseas to work on plantations in Brazil and mines in Mexico. Thirty percent of all African slaves came from Angola. Of those captured in the Angolan interior, only a quarter arrived alive on the other side of the Atlantic. In the three centuries of the Angolan slave trade, 12 million died.[4]
1536	First mineral prospectors arrive and proceed to tell Europe of fabulous riches. This prompts more expeditions, and the decision to take Angola by force of arms.
1571	"That the Kingdom of Angola be subjected and captured" — a royal order written in Lisbon. The formal conquest began in 1575; Luanda was founded in 1576 by the leader of the expeditionary force; and defeat for the Africans came about 100 years later.
1641	The Dutch, imperial competitors to the Portuguese for the lucrative slave trade, occupy Luanda and Benguela and strike alliances with the African powers. By 1648 they had withdrawn.

1700	Beginning of a stagnant century, Angola essentially serving as a labour pool for Brazil.
1820	First cotton plantations begun; they flourished, and at the time of the US civil war (1860 to 1865) there was a momentary boom, followed by collapse.
1834	Portugal decrees slavery illegal, but the slave trade continues for another 45 years, although no longer to Brazil.
1840	Penetration of the Angolan interior now of greater interest for commodity traders and planters. To secure the land, Portugal marshals expeditionary forces and 100 years of military action begins. Angolan resistance builds, but in the end is no match for the invaders' advanced firepower.
1869	Rubber is planted; it becomes Angola's number one export, reaching a peak in 1899, followed by collapse.
1899	Forced labour legally permitted, mainly to serve coffee and other plantation interests, and railway construction.
1902	Beginning of most intense period of African resistance and Portuguese military campaigns of subjugation, concluding about 1920. Foot soldiers were mainly local people, press-ganged and trained to fight. The Bakongo and Umbundo fought on for years.
1903	Benguela railway is begun; it was finished in 1929.
1906	Native poll tax is imposed, with the purpose of forcing Angolans to work for Portuguese.
1912	Discovery of diamonds.
1913	Present-day territory defined, Portuguese civilian authority replaces military command in most zones.
1920	Angolans now essentially "pacified" by military means.
1926	After 16 years of parliamentary rule, the military seize power in Portugal and establish the "New State", a fascist dictatorship, led from 1932 by Antonio Salazar.
1928	"Native Labour Code" is promulgated in Lisbon to permit press-ganging of African labour for mines, road-building, and plantations. Replaced by milder law in 1961 following uprisings by rural workers.
1950	Portuguese settlers, with government subsidies, begin arriving in large numbers. By 1960, settler population in coffee district of Uige is nearly six times larger than in 1950. Total settler population rises from 80,000 in 1950 to 350,000 in 1974.
1952	A group of 500 Angolan nationalists petition the United Nations to end Portuguese rule.

1953	Grouping of Luanda-based nationalists found the Party of the United Struggle of Africans of Angola (PLUA); this, together with others became the Movimento Popular de Libertação de Angola (MPLA) in December 1956. Major backing among black *assimilados,* mixed-race *mestiços,* and other urban classes, especially in Luanda and Malanje.
1957	Union of the Populations of North Angola, later UPA, founded by Bakongo grouping. In March 1962 this merged with others to form the Frente Nacional de Libertação de Angola (FNLA). Major backing to emerge among businessmen and prosperous Angolan coffee farmers.
1961	Plantation workers refuse to plant cotton in Malanje. MPLA attempts to free members held in Luanda prison; uprisings spread across northern coffee areas; 300 settlers killed. Portuguese reprisals leave more than 20,000 Angolans dead, with literate people special targets, as carriers of "the infections of nationalism."
1963	Organization of African Unity (OAU) recognizes FNLA's "government in exile" (acronym GRAE) in Kinshasa (then Leopoldville). FNLA comes to depend on patronage of President Mobutu of Zaire, and, through Mobutu, on United States financial support. MPLA sets up exile headquarters in Brazzaville, seeks international support, later comes to depend largely on Soviet Aid.
1964	Several Ovimbundu members of FNLA, including Jonas Savimbi, withdraw in protest alleging northern tribalism in FNLA. In March 1966 they found the União Nacional para a Independencia Total de Angola (UNITA); depended at first on support from China, then from South Africa from 1975 onward. Major following among Ovimbundu traders, farmers and labourers.
1965	MPLA begins small-scale guerrilla operations in Moxico province.
1968	Portuguese begin "hearts-and-minds" reform and "strategic villages" programmes in rural Angola. With Portugal enjoying US financial backing and NATO weapons supply, the military launch major offensives against MPLA in eastern Angola.
1969	OAU Liberation Committee notes that anti-colonial struggle in Angola is less intense than in Mozambique or Guinea. In 1971 the OAU withdraws recognition of GRAE as a spent force, and tries unsuccessfully to unite FNLA, UNITA and MPLA.
1970	Economic boom continues, with oil rapidly overtaking coffee and diamonds as main foreign exchange earner.
1973	All nationalist movements weakened and at low level of activity inside Angola. Soviets cut aid to MPLA, which turns for help to USA and elsewhere; US senior government officials refuse to assist.
1974	In April, Portuguese military officers in Lisbon end 48 years of fascist rule, and 13 years of financially and politically insupportable wars in Africa in which 11,000 Portuguese had died and 30,000 had been wounded. The coup leaders later indicate readiness to grant Angola independence under a coalition government of the three nationalist parties.

1975   January: Alvor Agreement signed by leaders of FNLA, MPLA, UNITA and Portugal setting 11 November as date of independence under a coalition government.

February: Breakdown of agreement. Beginning of what the MPLA terms the "Second War of Independence". FNLA and Zairean troops mount offensive backed by USA through the Central Intelligence Agency (CIA).

May: Cuba agrees to send military advisors and weapons to assist MPLA; Cuban forces arrive six months later.

July: after months of fighting, MPLA forces oust FNLA and UNITA from Luanda.

August: South African armed forces invade across Angola's southern border under several pretexts, including attacks on members of the Southwest Africa People's Organization (SWAPO). Major damage to towns, bridges and roads.

October: Heavily armed South African column advances on Luanda, halted by combined MPLA and just-arrived Cuban forces.

November: Last Portuguese troops depart on 10th, formal independence ceremony held on 11th, with Dr. Agostinho Neto, leader of the MPLA, sworn in as President of the People's Republic of Angola.

December: US Congress cuts off aid to UNITA and FNLA.

1976   February: Zairean and FNLA troops driven back into Zaire. US government authorizes Gulf Oil Company to release oil royalties, blocked since 1975, to new Luanda government. All subsequent US administrations refused to recognize the government, despite world-wide recognition and admission to all major international bodies.

March: South African troops and allies withdraw, leaving trail of destruction through southern Angola.

April: Angola and Cuba agree on reduction of Cuban forces which are reduced by more than one-third in less than a year. Increased South African Defence Force activity in southern border area stops any further Cuban withdrawal. US Congress, angered by revelations of covert operations and CIA cover-up, bans military aid to anti-government forces in Angola without congressional approval. Called the Clark Amendment, this law remained in force for nine years, until repealed in 1985.

1977   Attempted *putsch* by dissident MPLA group, involving mobilization of Luanda shantytown residents; it was put down quickly by MPLA and Cuban forces. Thereafter, MPLA shifted from a nationalist movement (with 110,000 card-carrying members up to 1977) to a Marxist-Leninist vanguard party (with only 15,300 members by 1980). Mass mobilization efforts of street and factory committees known as *Poder Popular* (People's Power), were wound up.

1979   President Neto dies; José Eduardo dos Santos, trained as a petroleum engineer, succeeds him.

1981   Ronald Reagan takes office as US President. Major South African military offensives begin in the south of Angola, together with support to UNITA; Cuban troops, as well as teachers and medical staff, begin arriving in larger numbers.

1983   In December the SADF launches Operation Askari, its biggest military operation of the period, surpassed only by the offensive against Cuito Cuanavale four years later. A better equipped Angolan army makes it the costliest SADF operation since 1975/76.

1984   A ceasefire plan, signed in Lusaka, Zambia between the Angolan and South African governments establishes a joint monitoring commission (JMC) to oversee withdrawal of South African troops. They do not withdraw but bargaining begins on withdrawal of Cuban troops.

1985   Major South African and Angolan government offensives begin with massive air, tank, artillery and conventional ground forces in eastern Angola as war escalates into high-technology, high-casualty confrontation.

1986   UNITA's financial and logistical support from the USA is increased and is openly announced after repeal of Clark Amendment the previous year.

1987   **August:** South Africa admits the SADF is in southern Angola assisting UNITA whose headquarters are threatened by a government offensive around Mavinga. Later in the year crack Cuban combat troops are committed to the fighting for the first time in 11 years. Previously protecting key installations and training government troops, the Cubans had not fired on the SADF since 1976.[5]

1988   **March:** The eight-month battle for Cuito Cuanavale ends with South African military withdrawal, creating friction between officers and politicians in Pretoria. This battle was the costliest for both sides in terms of lives lost and equipment destroyed. It marked a turning point in regional relations.

        December: Agreement reached between South Africa, Angola, Cuba and USA on Namibian Independence and Cuban withdrawal from Angola.

1989   President Mobutu of Zaire, under pressure from the US government, brings UNITA and MPLA leaders to peace talks in Gbadolite, Zaire. After generating superficial goodwill and a public relations triumph for Mobutu which enabled him to visit Washington, the ceasefire collapsed. Popular frustration towards both sides mounts in Angola.

1990   **April:** Peace talks between UNITA and the Angolan government begin in Portugal.

        December: MPLA's 700-strong Central Committee endorses multi-party system and autonomy for civil society.

1991   After seven rounds of negotiations in Portugal, a Peace Agreement is signed in Lisbon on 30 May by President dos Santos and UNITA leader Jonas Savimbi.

1992   Demobilization of military from both sides begins as does integration of 40,000 into a unified national force; electoral law is constituted, leading to registration of voters and internationally supervised elections in September.

Introduction

On 30 April 1991, representatives of the government of Angola and the UNITA guerrilla movement initialled documents in Lisbon, Portugal, leading to a ceasefire on 15 May and a formal Peace Agreement two weeks later on 30 May.

For Angola, beset by a cruel and devastating war all of its 16 years of independence from Portugal, these first steps toward peace were desperately needed and wholly unprecedented.

For the rest of the world, however, there *were* other parallels and precedents. Angola's was just one among a number of peace settlements in the early 1990s. Drawn-out wars, internally fought and externally propagated, known in military jargon as Low Intensity Conflicts, were coming to an end. In Nicaragua, El Salvador, Afghanistan and Cambodia peace was more urgent than anything else. In southern Africa, Namibia achieved its political independence from South Africa in March of 1990.

Each war was fought - and ended - in different ways. Each had its own particular roots. But it was no coincidence that these conflicts in poor countries of the South had been wound up at the same moment as the rich countries of the North were winding up their own cold war.

Indeed, the hot wars of the South and the cold war of the North seem so intimately related as to have been one and the same thing. That hypothesis must, finally, await the sifting and synthesizing of facts and ideas by historians and theorists of global politics.

This book has no such ambitions. Its focus is merely one case of a transition from war to peace — Angola's. And it treats only one dimension of that case — the human dimension.

Light shed on that relatively limited field may well illuminate part of the wider canvas of world history. Our aim here is to illuminate Angola for its own sake, its own struggle. It is people who, after all, live there: people with ordinary feelings and failings; people with human needs and capacities; people made extraordinarily vulnerable by war and economic distress.

One reason the Angolan people's ordeal merits special attention is that they endured it almost entirely on their own. Unlike other countries beset by war or natural disaster, where hundreds of millions of dollars and regiments of relief and aid workers have arrived to support the victims, Angola has received relatively little humanitarian assistance.

In similarly war-ravaged Mozambique, for example, foreign donors loom large, posing questions of who really calls the shots in that country.[1] During Angola's war such relationships of dependence and domination from relief and development agencies were hardly intense. True, Cuba provided a substantial amount of technical assistance: teachers, medical workers, scholarships and so on. A few Northern donors have stood by Angola down through the years. But in the main, it was the people who kept themselves going by relying on their own strength, their own ingenuity, their own instincts for survival.

Angola was badly battered by war. It was the theatre of some of the heaviest conventional warfare in the world outside the Middle East. There were regular military invasions by the most powerful army in Africa — the South African Defence Force (SADF). Guerrilla warfare pervaded the entire country. Hundreds of thousands perished and as many more were maimed and scarred by conflict. The breakdown of the economy put yet more people at risk.

But there is also another story. What merits attention and explanation — and admiration — are rates of survival well above what might have been expected in such an impoverished and distorted country.

This book grew out of a concern to expose both the devastation of 16 years of war and economic disruption, and also to look at the human responses of Angolans to that violence and disorder. It has been drawn together primarily to inform non-Angolans about one of the longest of the Cold War's armed conflicts on the world's periphery.

However, it will also serve as a mirror for Angolans to see their own country's ordeals, how their own men, women and children coped, and what are the challenges they face now that peace is slowly taking root in the rich soil of that astoundingly beautiful and strong nation.

Most of these pages are devoted to what Angolans themselves have experienced and what Angolans say about those experiences. Contributing throughout the book, is the work of a number of Angolan journalists and researchers whose writings were specially commissioned for the task during the first half of 1992. They are presented by name in the Acknowledgements.

Facts and views were sought from persons in, or associated with, a number of political streams in Angola. UNITA provided information and authorized a visit by a journalist to UNITA-held territory in the provinces of Huambo and Bie. Materials collected by others about UNITA- dominated zones have been consulted extensively.

Those associated with new political parties and formations were consulted extensively, as were members of the MPLA and the government of Angola. Indeed, government representatives, including the Ministry of Defence, provided important and hitherto confidential information. Angolan periodicals have been mined both for specific events of the post-ceasefire period as well as for the undercurrents of debate.

Non-Angolan sources, both individuals and international agencies, especially those with in-depth knowledge of socio-economic issues, were also consulted, and some non-Angolan writers were commissioned to pursue specialized topics.

This book is, however, Angolan in its essence. By far the greatest part of the facts and opinions presented in these pages derive directly from Angolan sources.

Statistical information about Angola is rarely precise and almost never comprehensive. Social scientists have long warned planners and economists in all situations about the shortcomings of data in both rich and poor countries.[2]

In the case of Angola, the warning is especially appropriate. Under the Portuguese, most Angolans had good reason to deny the authorities full, or even accurate, knowledge about themselves and their possessions. For example, the last official census, taken in the closing years of the colonial period, is therefore open to serious question. All surveys of national scope date from that period. Data from one such survey, on Angolan agriculture, still serves as a basis for policy — yet even its colonial makers held that its margin of error was plus or minus 25 percent! Since the early 1970s, war and disruption have made accurate surveys impossible.

A basic fact about Angola, then, is that it is barren in facts. Therefore, it is a difficult place in which to begin planning — a major impediment along the path to recovery.

This also makes it a difficult place to describe with a whole picture. The reader is invited to keep this caveat in mind, as have the writers, when perusing quantitative data about this land of smoke and mirrors.

1

The Legacy of War: Departures and Homecomings

The place: Estatamela, a little town on the central highlands. The time: late 1991.

A woman rushes to embrace her brother. "I am so happy my family has returned and is back together," she says, tears streaming down her face.[1]

Scenes like this took place daily across most of Angola in the emotional days following the ceasefire. Brothers, sisters, entire families came home in all corners of the country, wondering, worrying about what they might find.

Peace brought an end to exile and estrangement stretching back years, even lifetimes. War had begun to fling people away from the centres of their lives in the early 1960s. With growing centrifugal force, it sent them into the bush, across international frontiers and to the edges of towns and cities. Before it ended, war had displaced millions.

As with poor civilians in all 20th-century wars, it exhausted them and sharpened their demands for peace and order to come from the chaos.

Studies of poor people's letters during World War I in Europe, for example, indicate that "The fundamental theme in the correspondence of the poor was war as a disruption and destruction of *the order of life and labour*. Consequently the desire to return to a decent, orderly life increasingly implied hostility to war, to military service, to the war economy, etc. and the wish for peace."[2]

It was the same for Angolans in their 16-year war.

To review the prospects for restoring order and stability in daily lives, we must consider those made so vulnerable by the times in which they lived: the displaced, especially women and children, who fled from war and economic distress; and the young soldiers who had to fight the war which aggravated that distress.

Where people went at first, and when, have generally always been known. But just how many moved, and what their later patterns or cycles of movement were, is much more difficult to ascertain.

Displaced People: Do the Figures Add Up?

Government and international agencies have produced annual data on people internally displaced *(deslocados)* and refugees beyond Angola's borders. These were needed to justify appeals for food and other help from abroad. They served a purpose, but their accuracy was hampered by war.

Refugee professionals say that in situations like Angola's, the majority of people forced to move are seldom recorded as displaced. In most crises, displaced people tend to fall back on that basic African safety net — the extended family or clan.

Unless there are good reasons for doing so — such as becoming eligible for emergency food handouts — dislocated people will not usually register with any authority, foreign or domestic. "Most [African refugees] are surviving by dint of their capacity to co-exist with locals under extremely difficult conditions," says a leading expert on refugees.[3]

Photo 1.1: *People wating for a lift at Lubango, Huila Province, to take them north. Roads were de-mined after the cease fire, but are full of potholes.*

Bearing this and other data-distorting factors in mind in the case of Angola, information must be approached with caution, and viewed as an order of magnitude rather than precise numbers.

Who Moved Where, and Why

Some people were forced to move in waves, others in steady trickles over many years. The first displaced Angolans of the modern era were those who escaped forced labour under the Portuguese during the settler period. By 1954, up to half a million Angolans — more than 10 percent of the population at the time — had fled the country, mainly to Zaire.

Sudden, large-scale movements of the population began in 1961. Settler reprisals, including aerial bombardment, sent an estimated 150,000 people streaming across Angola's northern border into Zaire. Others stayed inside the country, but lived a precarious existence in the bush.

Forced settlement by the Portuguese into "protected villages" similar to those used in Vietnam and Rhodesia further re-arranged the demographic map. In addition, thousands of labourers recruited in the central highlands began arriving at northern coffee farms to replace those northerners who had gone into hiding or exile.

Later in the 1960s, several thousand people from Angola's far eastern provinces began fleeing into Zambia and Zaire to escape fighting between MPLA guerillas and Portuguese troops.

Throughout the decade of the 1960s and into the early 1970s as many as five percent of Angola's rural population moved to the cities, accounting for about half of all urban growth in that period. Immigrants from Portugal accounted for much of the rest.[4]

The real tidal waves of displacement began with the upheavals of 1975 to 1976. Following the coup that toppled the fascist regime in Lisbon in 1974, and the decision of the new Portuguese leaders to relinquish their claims to overseas colonies, a whole series of events severely disrupted Angolan life for almost two decades.

First, and most shattering to the economy, was the sudden massive exodus of the country's skilled and semi-skilled Portuguese work force. Fears of retribution and of an uncertain future under a majority-led government, prompted panic among the settlers. Of the estimated 335,000 Portuguese civilians in 1974, less than 30,000 remained in 1976.

Second, warfare and local hostility sent many thousands of labourers on coffee and other plantations in the north back to the central highlands.

Third, warfare among the contending nationalist parties forced thousands more residents of northern provinces back into the bush, or across the border into Zaire.

Fourth, more than 350,000 people fled with defeated UNITA forces from the central highlands into the bush following the South African withdrawal in 1976. This was the only period in which major towns and cities underwent temporary net losses of population.

By the time shooting stopped and a semblance of calm had returned in 1977, about 150,000 people had died and more than a million — a sixth of the population of 1975 — had been uprooted, many of them permanently.

The next three years through 1980 were relatively calm. Guerrilla warfare diminished and military activity was largely restricted to the southern border area.

However, the new MPLA government felt obliged to force half a million rural residents into protected villages in the central provinces to separate them from UNITA guerillas. By early 1981, at least 10 percent of the Angolan population lived in these settlements, inherited from the Portuguese.[5]

People also began flowing to the cities again, despite the disappearance of industrial and other jobs.

This was also a time when Namibian refugees and SWAPO guerillas began to increase their presence on Angolan soil, provoking South African assaults against them, as well as against Angolan forces. Angola also found itself with up to a quarter of a million Zairean refugees, who had fled their country's own political troubles earlier in the 1970s.

The upheavals of the 1980s began in earnest in 1981. Figure 1.1 shows the numbers of displaced persons before and after the South African offensive of August 1981. Revival of UNITA's armed activities and MPLA counter-offensives generated further displacement. By 1987 nearly 700,000 people were officially displaced inside Angola.

Between July 1985 and late 1987, more than 110,000 Angolans had joined the estimated 282,000 already recorded in Zaire. In the same period, 25,000 went to Zambia to join more than 69,000 already there. An estimated 40,000 Angolans fled to Namibia. Thus at least 526,000 persons, or

Figure 1.1: *Numbers of Displaced Persons*

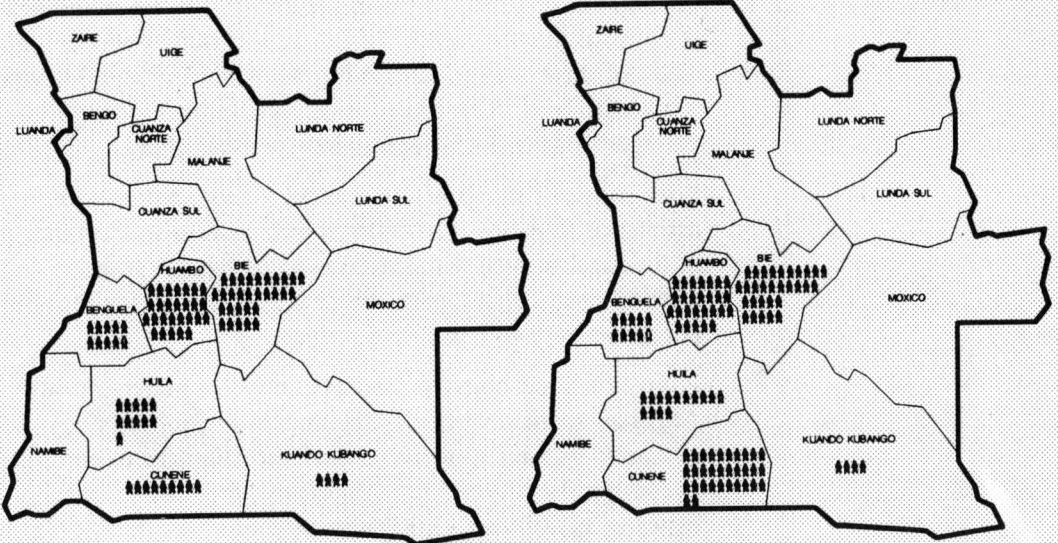

Concentration of displaced persons before (left) and after the
1981 South African Invasion (Operation Protea, selected provinces)

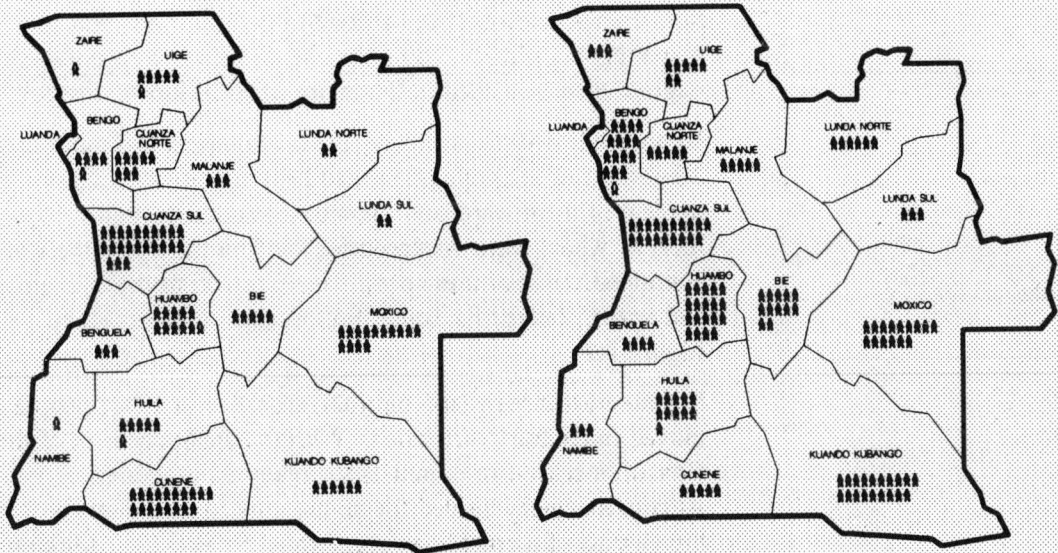

Concentration of displaced persons in 1987 (left) and
concentrations in 1990 (all provinces)

👤 5000 Persons   👤 Less than 5000 Persons

six percent of Angola's population, lived as refugees in neighbouring countries by late 1987.[6]

Vast stretches of the countryside were abandoned as movement to the dubious security of towns and cities accelerated. Many of these migrants were in the prime of life, leaving farming households short of able-bodied labour. One study of rural life in Malanje Province in 1988 found that up to two-thirds of the men and two-fifths of the women between the ages of 15 and 45 were no longer living there.[7]

With so many unproductive mouths to feed, and no real assistance from any other quarter, exhaustion was the daily lot of the rural women who stayed behind. Under such circumstances, it is remarkable that Angolan agriculture did not completely collapse.

Political and economic pressures compelled better-educated Angolans to go abroad. By the mid-1980s, job or study prospects had led up to 10,000 skilled Angolans to emigrate to Europe, Brazil or North America where they joined between 30,000 and 40,000 already there. As the fighting of the 1980s ground on, even more followed to escape the war, and conscription into the armies.

Angola's national university produced 764 graduates in the 10 years of Independence up to 1985, and many more degree-holders had returned from abroad to help in the vision of a new Angola. Yet in 1985 only 177 Angolans with university degrees were recorded in the entire national labour force.[8]

By the end of 1987, as many as 2 million persons, more than 20 percent of the population, had been uprooted. Eighty percent of them were adult women and children under 15, most of whom were displaced for the first time. As the war continued, most of these people were forced to move again and again. Indeed for some, life became nomadic. (See Figure 1.2)

For the next three years, until the ceasefire in 1991, people moved in contrary directions. With the announcement of the Gbadolite cease-fire in mid-1989, many thousands of Angolans eagerly headed for home, only to find they had been the victims of a cruel hoax perpetrated by President Mobutu for his own political gain.

From 1985 through 1988 some 60,000 to 80,000 Angolans affiliated with the FNLA, which had met defeat in the 1975-76 struggle, emerged from exile under terms of a Luanda government amnesty. Mostly Kikongo-speakers, many of them ended up in Luanda and main provincial towns.

For the 1980s as a decade, the government recorded the return of 120,000 refugees.

Meanwhile, the internally displaced — the *deslocados* — grew in number and misery. The policy of the registering agency, the State Secretariat for Social Affairs (SEAS), was to keep *deslocados* on official lists, and thus eligible for food relief, for only six months. Thereafter, the policy-makers reasoned, they were to become self-sufficient. Occasionally this rule was bent, and a few *deslocados* became semi-permanent wards of state charity.

Figure 1.2: *Movement of Displaced Persons*

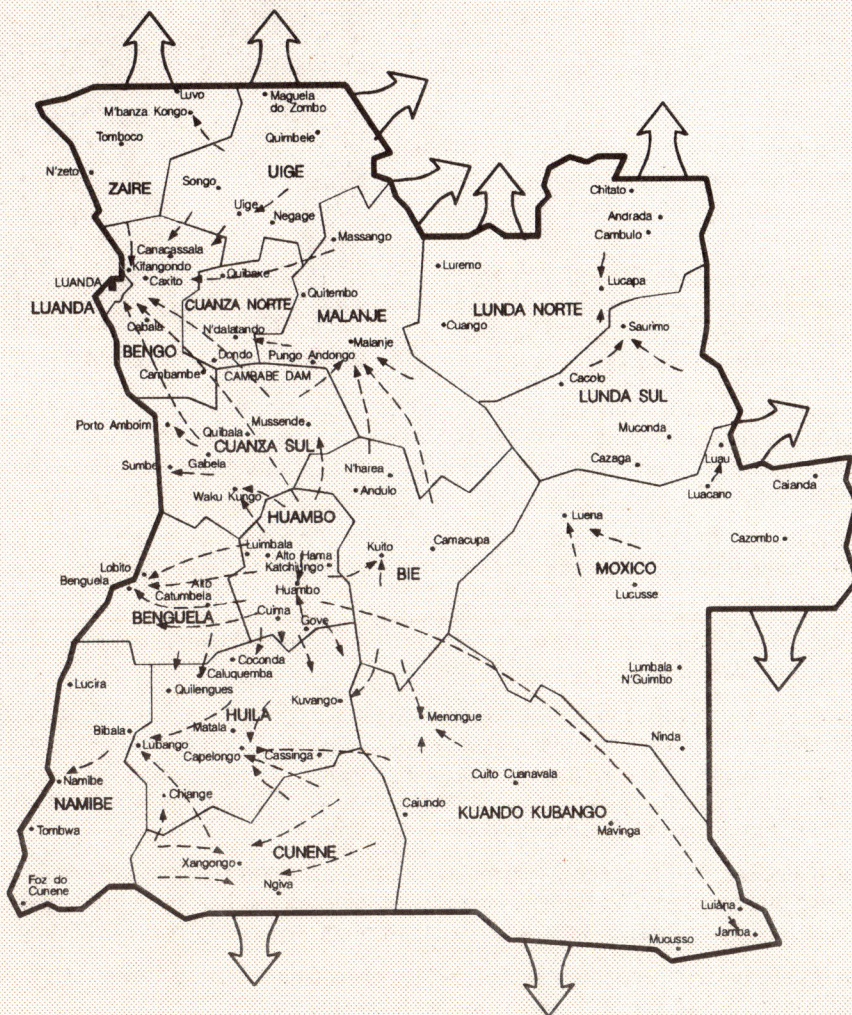

But in most cases SEAS adhered to its rule so official figures of displaced persons represent more a *flow* of persons than an *accumulation* of the permanently internally displaced. That accumulated number of *deslocados* likely reached between 1 million and 1.5 million people.

Estimates of the displaced populations in Moxico and Kuando Kubango provinces in the southeast varied considerably.

Surviving by Staying Put

"It is painful to tell about our life. We are living so badly." Chief Francisco Antonio Gomes, 74, speaks openly — and bitterly.

He is of the Province of Malanje, resident on an old settler farm, Fazenda Holanda. It is just seven kilometres from the construction site of the Capanda hydroelectric dam, a colossal and economically dubious project which even the state-owned newspaper recently termed "pharaonic".[9]

About 500 people live on the farm. Most are children and old people like the chief. The young people left during the war to live in Malanje town, Ndalatando and Luanda.

"We are trying to scrape by and make do with what the farm can produce," says the chief. "We have maize, beans, eggplant, potatoes and watermelon. We're peasants and we plant all our food."

Photo 1.2: *Chief Fransisco Antonio Gomes*

The community faces many shortages, just as it always has during the war years. Salt, sugar, and cooking oil are rarely seen. Clothes and shoes are few and costly. People would like to build or improve their houses but there are no zinc roofing sheets. There are no buses or trucks serving the people of the farm.

Before the war more than a thousand people stayed here. "We lived well then," Chief Francisco recalls. "We had our fields." Tenants sold their surpluses either to the landlord, or in the nearby town of Pungo Andongo.

"With the war, the owners of the farm returned to Holland. They lost everything they left behind," recalls the chief. "The war destroyed many things."

Countless times the people had to flee into the bush to escape the fighting. For long periods of time — "up to six months" — there would be no support from outside. "Our food was cassava meal with beans, *macunde* beans, *quizaca* beans and *borduega* beans. It wasn't possible to hunt. You couldn't go far into the bush. So we stayed put on the farm. Some help came from Pungo Andongo, which got help from Cacuso. But we could never count on it."

For lack of a teacher, the local school closed in 1984. Four years later the authorities at Pungo Andongo sent two teachers and the school reopened, offering the first three primary grades for about 50 students. The pupils just listen and watch; there are no teaching materials for any of them.

The old chief used to travel, especially in the 1940s, to Luanda and Malanje town. But from 1976 to 1991 he stayed put on the farm, and so came through the war.

During most of the 1980s, government forces held the few towns in this huge empty zone, while UNITA held the countryside. A US State Department researcher, visiting Kuando Kubango under UNITA auspices in 1989, estimated a population between 800,000 and 1 million, of whom as many as 85 percent were displaced.[10] Government data, on the other hand, showed a total 1990 population of only about 600,000, of whom just 17 percent were displaced. Only as voter registration proceeds this year will the actual truth of the matter be revealed.

By 1991, official figures from SEAS (which never counted displaced persons in Luanda) came to 900,000 *deslocados*. However, this almost certainly under-estimated the true total of people living away from their homes.

Following the May 1991 cease-fire, Angolans again started moving in large numbers. Exactly how many may never be known, since most of those moving did so without assistance. Although some received help from relief agencies, most returned spontaneously. UN situation reports and newspaper stories told of unexpectedly swift homecomings:

- "Kwanza Norte province: Refugee and internally displaced Angolans returning to their homes in province at faster rate than originally foreseen..."

- "Some 5,988 Angolans returned spontaneously from Zairean Republic between July and October [1991]".[12]

- "8,104 Angolans coming from Zaire welcomed in the Province of Uige from October to March."

- "1,500 Angolans returned during the first two weeks of January [1992, to Bengo Province]".[13]

- "Cunene authorities reported over 9,000 persons returned to their original communities.[14]

Surveys among refugees — some 300,000 in Zaire and 100,000 in Zambia — showed that three-quarters wished to return home. Since all returnees over 18-years-old were potential voters, political party pressures mounted for — and against — their speedy return in time for registration.

However, conditions to transport and receive them were clearly inadequate. Some refugees knew that, and stayed put. By mid-1992 it was clear that only a portion of those in exile would be present and entitled to vote in Angola's first election.

Social prejudices also bedevilled some returnees, especially those coming back from Zaire. They were sometimes labelled "foreigners" and made to feel unwelcome, even though they are Angolan citizens in good standing. The injustice was compounded when they saw the problem-free welcomes accorded Angolans returning from Portugal and elsewhere. As in so many other countries, Angola is only slowly changing from a crucible of ethnic resentments to a melting-pot of ethnic assimilation and social harmony.

Movement from urban areas back to the countryside was observed among those on the edges of small towns in rural zones. Some old people decided to move back to their villages for the remaining years of their lives. But younger households established in the big cities during the war years remained there. Trade between countryside and city remains tilted decisively in favour of the urban.

Towns and Cities: Home to the Permanent Refugees

Urban areas became sanctuaries during the war. Life in cities and towns was difficult and dangerous, but it was better by far than the terror and misery of life in the countryside.

The war accounted for some, but by no means all, of the growth of Angola's urban population. During the colonial period, as in many colonies, the imperatives of growth made labour quite mobile. Angola's main cities began growing rapidly in the 1940s. Luanda's growth, which entailed massive immigration from Portugal, was estimated at seven percent per annum in the period 1940-1970. (See Figure 1.3)

Several countries in southern Africa have undergone such transitions in gradual stages. But Angola's was a forced march. In the short space of 40 years, Angolan life shifted from one based in tiny, dispersed agrarian settlements to one based in urban centres.

In 1950, towns and cities (that is, settlements of more than 5,000) accounted for only 5.5 percent of the population; by 1990, about half the population lived in urban areas.

Some government planning documents are now based on an urban population (in the broad sense) making up 60 percent of the total population.

Between 1976 and 1992, internal migration accounted for most of this growth. Natural rates of increase, though important, were secondary. One estimate is a shift of 600,000 persons to urban areas due to war. Complementing this is an estimate of 450,000 moving to Luanda alone between 1970 and 1990.[15]

Today, one of the most serious problems facing the cities is that they were built to accommodate less than a fifth of the people now requiring clean water supplies and other public services. Huambo, for example, was built for 70,000 persons. During the war, it became home to six times that many people. Almost as dramatic has been the growth of Benguela and Lobito, Lubango and Malanje.

Some of the growth is immediately visible in the extensive, unregulated neighbourhoods of the poor, which now encircle most urban areas. Through these spontaneous settlements, Angolan cities have become both more crowded and more sprawling. In some of Luanda's older shantytowns, 800

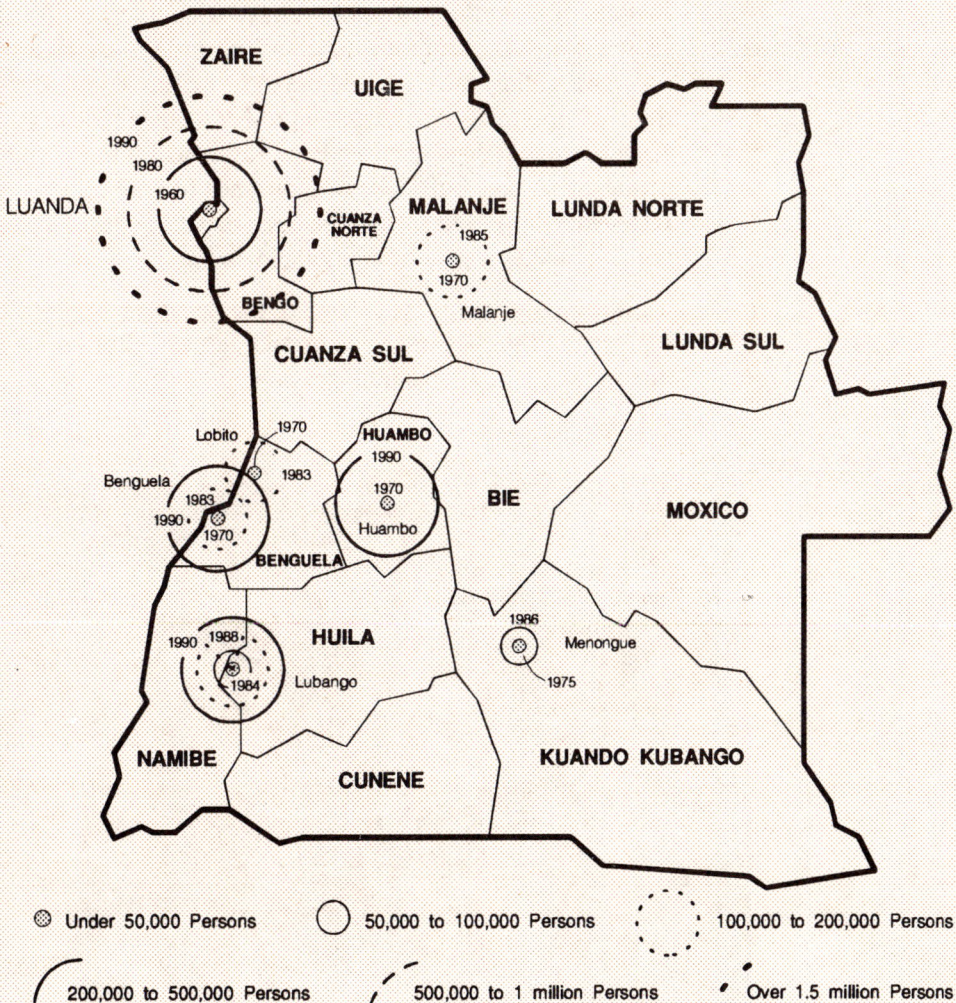

Figure 1.3: *Growth of Cities*

Legend:
- Under 50,000 Persons
- 50,000 to 100,000 Persons
- 100,000 to 200,000 Persons
- 200,000 to 500,000 Persons
- 500,000 to 1 million Persons
- Over 1.5 million Persons

persons per hectare could be found by the mid-1980s — human densities seen only in Asia.

Such overcrowding is manageable if people are encouraged, equipped and organized to handle it, but in Angola this has yet to occur. The result is squalor, appalling levels of crime and social breakdown, dangerous overcrowding (three or four persons sleeping in one room), no running water close at hand and an overflowing pit latrine nearby. This is the norm in Luanda's poor neighbourhoods. A third of the population there lives in shacks or huts, while many more live in mud-brick or cement-brick houses in poor states of repair, and with no protection against mosquitoes.[16]

Yet the poor sections of Angolan cities have seen little, if any, public investment in water, sanitation, or drainage. What few improvements have occurred are those taken by residents themselves on their own initiative.

In spite of everything, Angolans have tried to create decent lives for themselves in the cities. With little more than their own sweat, they have created the most massive, and arguably the most impressive construction to have taken place in Angola since Independence. Poor residents on the peripheries of the cities have built tens of thousands of houses, latrines, little workshops and storage places — such modest buildings are concrete evidence of energy and saving.

They are poor things, but they are the occupant's own. They represent a fight against squalor and despair. But on balance, that fight is still far from being won.

Photo 1.3: *Displaced persons on the move.*

Encampments and the Demobilized

In Angola's Peace Accords, the greatest detail and precision is devoted to the fighting forces, especially where they had to go and by what dates. The plan gave both sides 60 days in which to move their respective forces to 49 assembly points or *acantonamentos*, as well as 32 ports and border posts. Demobilization was to follow.

Actually, it took 300 days until late March 1992, before demobilization began. And even then only two-thirds of the 160,000 originally expected in the assembly points actually turned up. Since many of non-appearing soldiers were thought to be carrying firearms, this was an unsettling development. But because earlier estimates may have been based on figures inflated for political purposes, it is not known just how many no-show soldiers there were.

The Deslocados: Survival

Following is an excerpt from a report by a Dutch foundation official about his visit to a displaced persons camp at Kuvango, in eastern Huila province, in April 1988:[11]

"Kuvango has in fact three groups of displaced persons:

1. the 2,000 recently-arrived refugees from Galangue temporarily housed in the barracks on the edge of the town;

2. the 600 displaced persons who arrived last August and have been resettled eight kilometres north of Kuvango town; and

3. the other 1,360, who live in the 'Transit' and 'Permanent' settlements.

"The 600 displaced persons who, when I visited last year in September, still had to sleep under the open sky, have in the meantime built up a whole village with a school and a health post, albeit a primitive one. Although not every family yet has its own house, and there are some shared communal lodgings, that shouldn't last much longer since building activity was in full swing with the end of the rainy season.

"Twenty-six hectares of land had been put under cultivation of maize and beans, sufficient for four months' supply, as well as some potatoes for sale. These had generated 60,000 kwanzas which were used to repay the government for the seed supplied. Meanwhile tomato and onion seedlings have been started, which will be planted after the maize and beans are harvested. To put more land under cultivation, more oxen and plows are needed.

"Seven months ago, I met here a beaten-down, almost apathetic, group of refugees who were tired, hungry and sick, who had lost all their goods and were obliged to sleep under the open sky. Now we see energetic and cheerful people who again have some confidence in life...and have begun to build a new future.

"It was otherwise with the 2,000 refugees from Galangue, who had arrived three weeks earlier after an attack on their village in Kuvango *município* and were temporarily housed in the barracks. These people had been hit hard by what the war had dealt them, and their days of flight through the bush in which 35 people lost their lives....[This is a] typical example of the disastrous situation to which the war in Angola leads."

Assembling Angola's soldiers was a tricky and demanding job. The responsibility rested with the Joint Verification and Monitoring Commission *(Comissao Mista de Verificação - CMVF)* composed of government and UNITA members, with Portuguese, US and Russian observers.

Monitoring the processes were members of UNAVEM II — the United Nations Angola Verification Mission, involving 350 military observers, 90 police observers and 250 support staff. Four hundred more observers were to be added in 1992 for the election period.

More than 100 Portuguese, and a small number of British and French military staff also came on a variety of related assignments, including training and integration of a new national defence force.

Getting troops into the assembly points was an uneven and unsteady process. Recording it also involved some manipulation of numbers, as shown in Table 1.1.[17]

The numbers game began with the totals expected to show up. First, UNITA's troop strength was a third less than the 75,000 it had claimed toward the end of the war. The government figures were closer to established estimates of troop strength; in September 1991 its estimate was about 130,000, which was reduced by 15 percent by November.

Table 1.1: Forces in Assembly Points (November 1991 to March 1992)

Expected: According to Government and Unita Sources

	Number of Troops		
	November 1991	February 1992	March 1992
Government	110 140	109 100	101 756
UNITA	49 700	37 230	37 330
Totals	159 840	146 330	139 086
Actual Counts: Verified by UNAVEM II Observers*			
Government	73 830 (67%)	65 124 (60%)	65 419 (64%)
UNITA	31 973 (64%)	35 143 (94%)	35 061 (94%)
Totals	105 803 (66%)	100 267 (69%)	100 480 (72%)

* Values in parentheses indicate percent of expected values which were verified.

Second, the projected numbers began to drop when commanders realized that the troops were not forthcoming. If the original projections had been kept as the official benchmark, then only about 68 percent of government soldiers would have been accounted for, at one time or another, and about 71 percent of UNITA soldiers.

But between 31 October 1991 and 13 February 1992, 12,637 government troops had gone AWOL (Absent Without Official Leave) representing one-sixth of all those counted on 31 October 91. By contrast UNAVEM II records no single case of a UNITA soldier going AWOL during this period.

Why the difference? First, UNITA troops were generally assembled in their home areas with wives and children close at hand as is the case with guerilla armies; this was rarely the case with government soldiers. Moreover, informed UN observers suggested that the government had failed to pay many of its troops, sometimes for long periods. Later the government did not succeed in organizing the regular supply of food to the assembly areas. Not only did government troops go AWOL, they protested the lack of food and logistical support. There may have been deeper reasons at play, among them the soldiers' own aspirations, as suggested by a survey of their backgrounds and hopes. (See Box on Troop Background, page 20.)

The first formal demobilizations took place in late March 1992. Among the first were government and UNITA assembly areas in Huila Province, where 360 troops were discharged. Each

Photo 1.4: *An assembly point for government soldiers, 16 kilometres from Lubango, where about 2,000 troops were gathered following the ceasefire.*

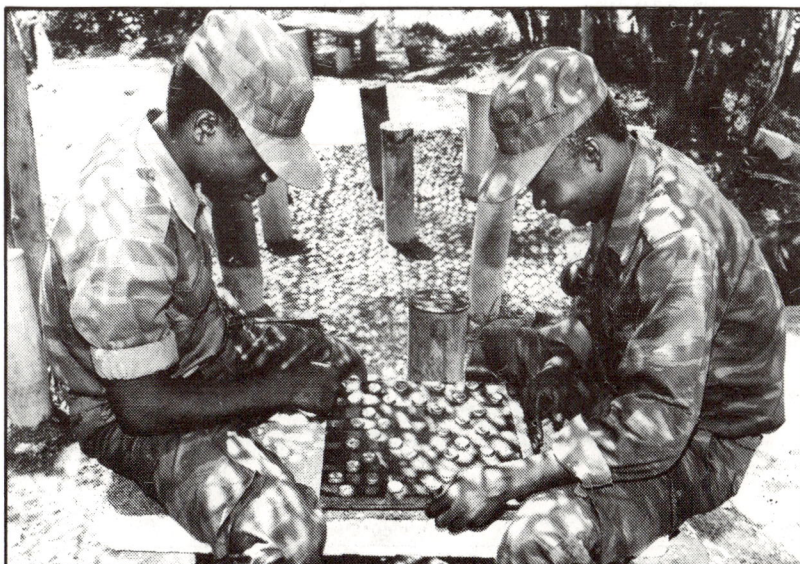

Troop Background

Who were Angola's combat troops during the war? And what did they aspire to? A written survey of over 77,000 government soldiers in late 1991 showed that respondents overwhelmingly (84 percent) wished to follow vocational or professional training courses.[18]

Less is known about UNITA soldiers. A survey carried out by UNITA covered only those to be demobilized. In the fragmentary findings available from that study, the most striking point was the high proportion saying they wanted to farm (38.4 percent) and to get into commerce (23 percent) after demobilization. Government soldiers expressed far less interest in these occupations.

Table 1.2: Survey of Troops

Age	18 to 21	20 percent
	22 to 25	34 percent
	26 to 30	31 percent
	31 and over	15 percent
Military Service	Less than 1 year	4 percent
	1 to 3 years	20 percent
	4 to 5 years	21 percent
	6 to 10 years	44 percent
	11 years and over	11 percent
Provinces of Birth	Benguela/Huambo/Bie	30 percent
	Huila/Namibe/Cunene	16 percent
	Luanda	7 percent
	Malanje/Kwanza Sul/Kwanza Norte/Bengo	30 percent
	Uige/Zaire/Cabinda	9 percent
	Lundas/Moxico/K. Kub.	8 percent
Schooling	Illiterate	1 percent
	1 to 4 class	38 percent
	5 to 6 class	38 percent
	7 to 8 class	17 percent
	Technical/higher	6 percent
Background Before Joining Army	Student	19 percent
	Auto mechanic	6 percent
	Farmer	4 percent
	Construction worker	3 percent
	Teacher	2 percent
	Mechanic	2 percent
Preferred Occupation (Main Examples)	Driver	17 percent
	Auto mechanic	12 percent
	"Agriculture"	9 percent
	"Health"	7 percent
	Construction	5 percent
	Commerce/business	5 percent
	Public administration/service	5 percent
	"Electricity"	3 percent
	Posts and telecommunications	2 percent
	"Industry"	2 percent
	Electronics	1 percent
	Police, etc.	0.2 percent
	No preference	8 percent

received 180,000 kwanzas (about US$100), equivalent to five months' pay, some items of clothing and an "availability passport" *(passaporte de disponibilidade)*, presumably to show prospective employers or schools. Costs of their transport home were also met by the government.

Journalists talking with the demobbed soldiers found happy young men, but few of them with concrete plans for the future. Rather, behind the relief at being discharged there were deep worries about the future. At Camitongo assembly point in Moxico, one ex-government soldier, speaking on behalf of his mates at the demobilization ceremony referred to the "enormous army of the unemployed" which they were about to join.[19]

Governmental and non-governmental organizations drew up plans for training in mechanics, electrical repair and maintenance, construction, administration and farm management. In a first phase, 20,000 ex-fighters would be schooled in 37 state vocational training centres. There was a

Soldiering On

Mario Mastelo, 32, has been fighting with UNITA's military machine half his life. Fighting is all he has known since 1976. "Living in the bush and suffering taught me how to survive," he says. Originally from the Municipio of Andulo in Bie Province, he has no profession beyond that of a guerilla fighter.

In February 1992 Mario was one of 2,200 UNITA troops waiting at the Cambandua Assembly Point some 40 kilometres east of the Bie provincial capital, Kuito. Before the war, Cambandua was a typical small trading centre. Today it is level with the ground; where shops and a school once stood, all is rubble.

UNITA soldiers deny any destructive effects of their presence. "The areas liberated by UNITA did not abandon their traditions," says former UNITA fighter, Kawango Hopoti Sepalanga. "The people living under government control felt oppressed. They were satisfied and cooperated with UNITA's control." The same sentiments were heard from other soldiers at Cambandua.

Whatever the truth of that statement, there was visible evidence of UNITA's efforts to win local support. For next to the ruins of Cambandua, UNITA members had set up some services. Out of the heaps of broken bricks its members had built a small health post, staffed by UNITA medics. A school and meeting huts made of poles and thatch have also had been constructed. The centre's one thriving business concern was a mill, powered by a diesel motor, for grinding local farmers' maize into flour.

Perhaps for this reason Mario Mastelo shows confidence in the promises of his party's leader. "Our strong head will provide us with opportunities to train if we leave the army," he says.

But he may not have to quit the army life. Together with the 35,000 other UNITA soldiers facing demobilization, Mario's chances of remaining a soldier were better than that of any of his 66,000 government army compatriots. For 20,000 from each force were to be selected to create a new defence force in the unitary Armed Forces of Angola. Soldiering is perhaps all Mario will know in life, and, with luck, the rest will be peacetime soldiering.

proposal to meet some demobilization costs through special taxes on the state's lucrative lottery and football pools.

In a bid to recover Angola's run-down conservation areas, over 800 demobilized soldiers are to be recruited and trained for work as game scouts, forest rangers, and national park support staff under Angola's National Forestry Department, funded by the International Union for the Conservation of Nature (IUCN).

Meanwhile the government spoke of public works employment, especially to repair damaged roads. UNITA officials quietly promised "jobs for the boys". One senior government official spoke of settling ex-combatants on abandoned farms, as was done in Zimbabwe, after its liberation war.

These intentions may be sound and logical: a country physically and economically flattened by war could well be built up again by the strong backs of those who fought the war. But such intentions bump up at once against Angola's poorly-developed means to organize and manage such undertakings.

In the short term, most ex-combatants are going to have to make their own way, regardless of what may be promised.

Point II.3 of the Cease-fire Agreement stipulated the release of all civilian and military prisoners held because of the war, but set no deadlines. And neither side seemed to be in any hurry to free its captives. By mid-February 1992, UNITA had released 3,983, while the government had released 940 prisoners, according to the International Committee of the Red Cross, the official monitor in the issue of prisoners. Accusations that the government held thousands of UNITA soldiers and sympathizers were countered by claims that UNITA was holding up even more people against their will in its forest headquarters at Jamba. The truth of these accusations was in considerable doubt, as both sides used the issue to score political points against the other. But the basic fact remained that many people were held against their will long after the end of hostilities.

2

Human Losses: The Tragedy of the War

On battlefields and rural roads, in farmers' huts and children's wards, war brought death to hundreds of thousands of Angolans. It left countless others physically and psychologically crippled. It spared no age, no ethnic group, no region. Nor did it leave social institutions and national culture untouched. Parts of Angola's rich environment were badly degraded. Altogether, the war seriously compromised the future of the country.

In total, about 900,000 Angolans died.

Of these, 85 to 95 percent were non-combatants, mainly children and infants. Since the average age of combatants was about 22, one conclusion is obvious: Angola's war devoured both its children and its youth.

The Cost in Human Lives

As in any war, the total losses of the Angolan conflict between 1975 and mid-1991 will never be known with great precision. How many died and how many had their lives broken can only be estimated.

Life-saving improvements in public health and nutrition began to collapse, leaving a large, uncountable number of victims who might otherwise have lived. They perished for lack of food, public hygiene and medical care.

There are essentially two categories: victims of direct hostilities, and victims of war's secondary effects.

Government sources put the Angolan death toll on both sides for the 16 years of war at 120,621 direct victims of the fighting. (See Figure 2.1)

The major shortcoming of these figures is that they refer only to hostile actions *against* government forces and civilians by

Figure 2.1: *Summary of Dead and Injured*

Government Troops: Dead and Injured

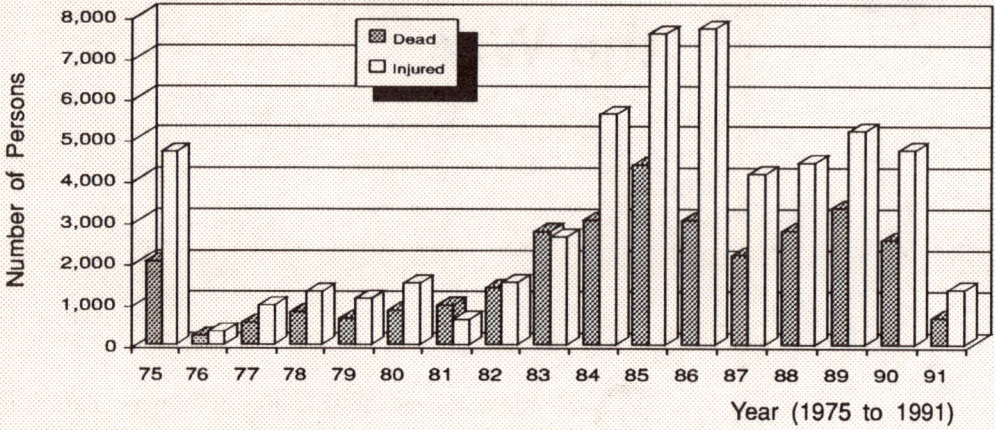

Non-Government Troops: Dead

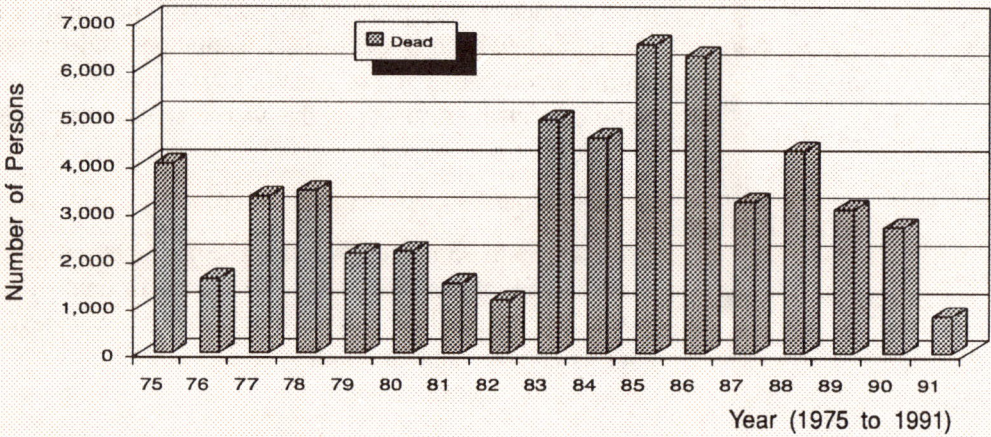

Civilians: Dead and Injured

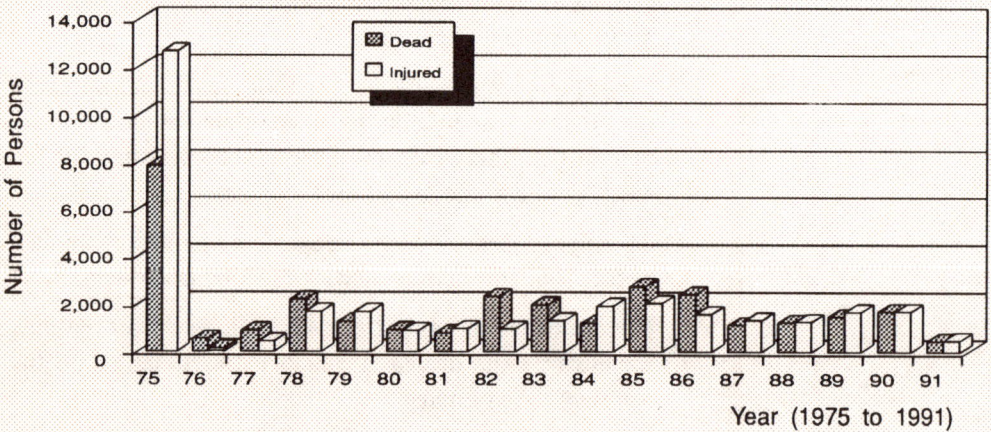

Note: Figures for injured non-Government troops not available.

UNITA and other opponents of the Angolan government. Not included, therefore, are losses incurred in operations *initiated by* government forces and their Cuban allies. For example, losses in major government offensives around Mavinga in 1985 — among the bloodiest of the war — are not included. Government military losses presented here are almost certainly under-estimates.

Secondly, civilian war deaths inaccessible to government estimators are not included due to the impossibility of verifying these casualties.

Horrendous as it is, the total count of direct war deaths presented here almost certainly under-states the true total.

Who died among government forces? Information from the government's Military Command *(Estado Maior Geral)* indicates that 91 percent were ordinary foot soldiers, although these constituted a smaller proportion (about 68 percent) of all forces. Commissioned and non-commissioned officers suffered lighter casualties. As in any war, the higher one's rank, the better one's chances of survival.

Civilian deaths and injuries were not recorded by age or gender, but a broad rule of thumb in Angola is: 40 percent children, 30 percent women, 30 percent men.

The information shown in Figure 2.1 is roughly congruent with post-war estimates by the Ministry of Health of 70,000 amputees, which includes both military and civilian victims.[1]

How and when did casualties occur? From Ministry of Defence sources, one picture is available. This is shown in Figure 2.2 of actions carried out by the government's opponents. They do not include the government forces' own actions.

Indirect Victims

Many more people died of preventable illness and hunger than died as a result of armed action. Acute diarrhoeal diseases (including cholera), malaria and respiratory tract infections, among other things, killed Angolans in increasing numbers during the war years. Children were the main victims. The war made them vulnerable by depriving them of food, clean water, medical services and simply loving care. As one farmer in Uige Province told a reporter, "It's sad to tell of what I saw in that period: children died like goats."[2]

A UN task force estimated in 1989 that as many as 90,000 adults and older children died from starvation, malnutrition and disease between 1980 and 1988. It went on to cite

Figure 2.2: *Breakdown of Deaths from War Actions*

Number of Persons

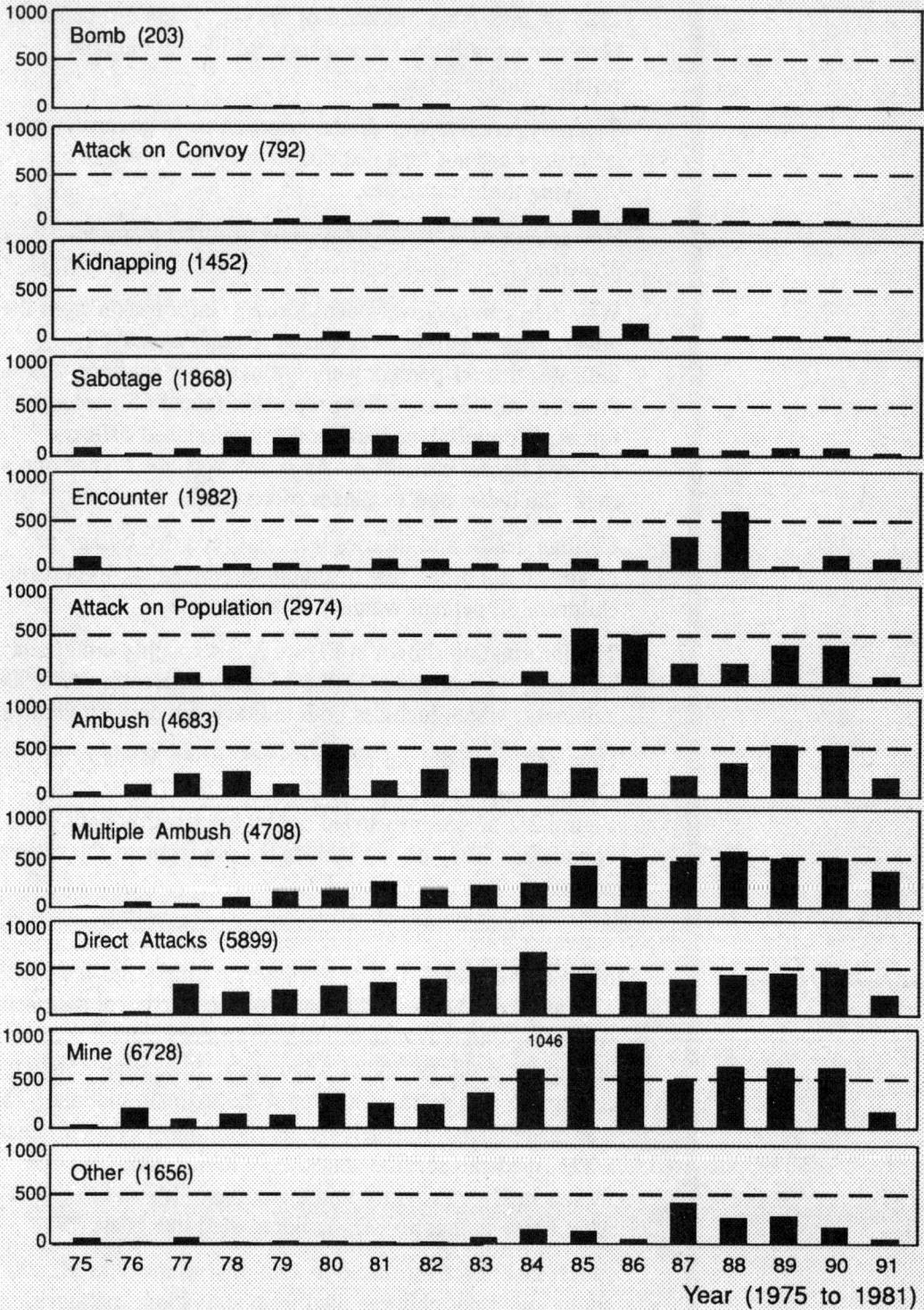

Bomb (203)

Attack on Convoy (792)

Kidnapping (1452)

Sabotage (1868)

Encounter (1982)

Attack on Population (2974)

Ambush (4683)

Multiple Ambush (4708)

Direct Attacks (5899)

Mine (6728)

Other (1656)

Year (1975 to 1981)

Note: Values in parentheses indicate total number of deaths due to type of attack.

UNICEF's calculation (based on a projected improvement of health indices to Tanzanian levels in the absence of war) that 331,000 children under five died in the same period.[3]

This means that by mid-1991 there were at least 485,000 indirect victims of the war under the age of five. By accepting the assumptions of UNICEF, and extrapolating the death rate another two-and-a-half years, we arrive at yet another example of the dreadful human costs of the war.

Further extrapolating the UN task force figures for deaths among adults and older children, it is estimated that 115,000 died in the period 1989 to mid-1991.

In the early post-independence period (1975 to 1979) deaths were not estimated on the same basis. However, one careful student of Angolan history suggests that some 150,000 people lost their lives from warfare, disease and malnutrition in the first year (1975-1976) alone.[4] The government estimates that 17,000 were killed just in the fighting of that year. Conservatively estimating those figures as valid for 1975-1979, and deducting government estimates of 17,000, then indirect victims in those first four years of war would be, at the very least, 133,000. (See Table 2.1)

It is reasonable, therefore, to assume that about 900,000 Angolans died as a result of 16 years of war.

Angola's population in 1975 was about 6.3 million, and in 1991 about 10 million. If a similar loss of life occured in the following countries over the same period, the numbers would be apocalyptic: in Canada, 2.4 million dead; France, 5 million

Table 2.1: Summary of Deaths (1975 to mid-1991)

Category	Dates	Deaths	Percentage of Total
All indirect deaths	1975 to 1979	133,000	16
Under-five indirect deaths	1980 to 1991	485,000	57
Over-five indirect deaths	1980 to 1991	115,000	13
Direct deaths: Combatants	1975 to 1991	88,000	10
Direct deaths: Civilians	1975 to 1991	32,000	4
Total Angolan deaths	1975 to 1991	853,000	

dead; Portugal, 900,000 dead; Sweden, 750,000 dead; United Kingdom, 5.1 million dead; US, 22.5 million dead.

The Sick, the Hungry

Diseases which would have been under control by the end of the 1980s had there been an absence of war, have persisted and in some cases spread because of the war. Table 2.2, based on the caseload at government health units in 1989, indicates the main illnesses of the war and how deadly they were.[5]

Similar figures of these tropical diseases could be found in other African countries. What makes Angola's so unusual is how persistent and lethal they have been. As a rule, such diseases are preventable and curable and in those African countries at peace, they are being brought under control.

Table 2.2: Estimated Deaths due to Illness (1989)

Type of Disease	Number of Cases (Thousands)	Deaths per Thousand
Malaria	806	5.6
Diarrhoea	348	14.6
Acute respiratory	238	6.1
Convulsive cough	20	7.8
Measles	19	92.4
Cholera	18	52.6
Bilharzia	17	1.7
Hepatitis	10	30.9
Tuberculosis	6	79.3
Filariosis	4	-
Gonorrhea	2	-
Neonatal tetanus	1	501.4
Tetanus (other ages)	1	260.7
Sleeping sickness	1	45.6
Meningitis	1	528.9

Angola was never allowed that peace.

Not shown above are trends, such as the alarming increase in deaths due to malaria which accounted for eight percent of all burials in Luanda cemeteries in 1985, but 19 percent in 1989.[6]

And, of course, behind such figures are unimaginable levels of human suffering. They indicate serious losses of human potential for creative, and especially productive, ends. Illness is a drain on people's lives, and a threat to their economic survival. A minor illness for a self-employed vendor, or her child, can mean a major loss of weekly income. Illness in a farming family at peak moments in the annual work cycle can mean hunger the following year.

Angola's war did not create these conditions, but it certainly helped worsen them, especially for already over-burdened women, who have to care for the sick. The best way for people to resist disease is, of course, primary health care in which good nutrition is one of the essential components. Here, too, the war made poor Angolans vulnerable.

In 1991 Angola had available for the population as a whole only 72 percent of their normal calorie requirements from basic foods. In 1981 that percentage had been 97.5 percent (up from 87 percent in 1970, in the colonial era).[7]

Such data are based on estimates of local production, probable imports and therefore food deficits in *basic food products* — cereals and tubers, etc. Over the years deficits have risen, according to these estimates. Some Angolans ate at adequate levels, but many did not.

Poor Angolans suffered acute and chronic under-nutrition during different periods of history, and in differing degrees. Studies show high levels of *stunting* (low height for age) among schoolchildren.[8] Acute malnutrition appeared, especially in zones of massive displacement of people and heavy fighting, such as in the southern reaches of the central highlands in the late 1980s.[9] Data from UNITA-held territory in Kuando Kubango Province tell much the same story.[10] People on the run, or trapped by the warfare swirling around them, suffered most.

Experts are still assessing the extent and the depth of malnutrition in Angola. The war put many people at serious risk by lowering their resistance to disease and it literally stunted the lives of many more, but Angolans survived in far greater numbers than food data suggests. (As Chapter 3 indicates, they had their own strategies for survival.)

Low Birth-Weight Babies

The proportion of babies with low birth weights is one of the key indicators of general nutrition. It is a better measure than calorie supply, since it shows results of actual food intake, as opposed to the estimated availability of food.

"Malnutrition in Angola begins even before birth. The percentage of babies whose weight was low at birth, i.e. weight below 2.5 kilograms, was approximately 20 percent for children born in lying-in clinics in 1986, which is indicative of the serious nutrition situation."[11]

Angola's average of 17 per cent in the period 1980-1988 is bad, but it is merely average for those countries classified by UNICEF in the very high child mortality group (over 140 per 1,000). Its low birth weight is better than those recorded in the same period in Malawi, Honduras and the Philippines and very much better than the rates recorded in Bangladesh.

Thus Angolans — at least pregnant women — have been feeding themselves better than what international comparisons of official statistics would suggest.[12]

Figure 2.3: *Percentage of Low Birth Weight Infants*

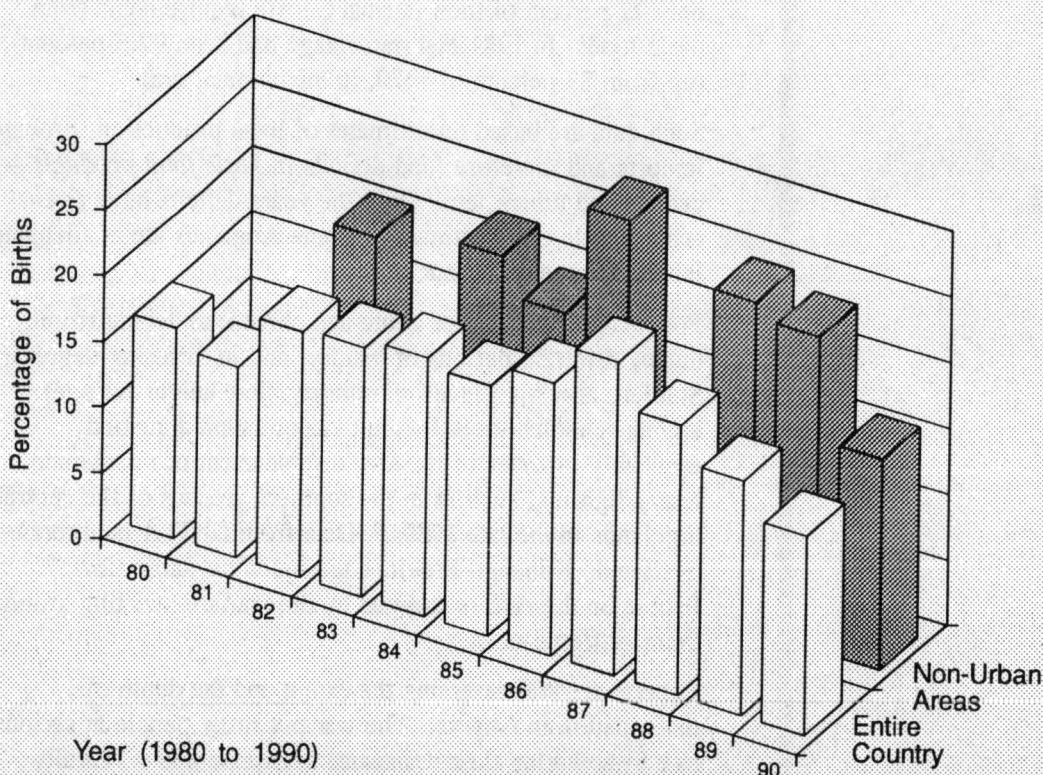

Children: The Orphaned and the Traumatized

The war shredded social safety nets with such violence that even children — for whom there is "always" a warm back to rest against, or a common pot from which to eat — were cast adrift.

By 1991 the government knew of at least 30,000 abandoned or orphaned children. Of these, some 4,000 were in state orphanages, 2,500 formally placed in foster care and a number were studying in Cuba. About 20,000 were at large, but uncounted. Thus Angola ended the war with about 50,000 orphans.[13]

Rarely, however, were abandoned and orphaned children alone. They found homes with other families, showing, as one close observer commented, "that even in situations of extreme poverty, feelings of solidarity are maintained."[14] Such arrangements have rescued thousands from total abandonment and a life on the streets.

Foster children in Angola are put to work, says the Director of the National Children's Institute, Goncalves Muandumba. "The most common situation is that the child is used by the family to take part in meeting the budget, and even more to take care of the house and young siblings, a traditional custom in the culture of less privileged strata."[15]

But the line between normal household tasks and exploitation is not clear, especially for girls. It is commonly assumed that foster children can become household slaves, with fewer rights than family children.

Angola's cities have always known some street urchins, but never in the numbers now seen. Some older children work the streets as petty traders, washing cars and shining shoes. They normally return home in the evenings. What is of growing concern are the younger children *living* in the streets, maintaining little, or no contact with family life.

"Some leave home not just to flee misery," says an Angolan specialist, "but also to escape the daily violence typical of a collapsing family. Those are parents with no definite calling, war-injured, or alcoholics who educate their children through violence and even rape."[16]

There was also the horror of war. Some children were victims of extreme aggression. Homes and villages were attacked. Families (or unaccompanied children) spent days and weeks in search of sanctuary. Orphanages, such as those in Moxico and Huambo provinces, were attacked.

Some of the most badly traumatized children found their way to orphanages, where their sleep is still broken by nightmares of fear of further attacks. In the Otchio orphanage in Lubango, for example, where over 200 children live, many suffer severe psychological scars. A resident specialist at Otchio said badly-affected children "do not fit in well with the other children in a family and the foster parents don't know how to handle the apathy and vandalism of the orphanage children."[17]

Focused, long-term programmes for young war-trauma victims of the kind seen in Mozambique have yet to appear in Angola. Thus, there are no similar surveys. Given the basic similarity of the terror tactics used in both wars, it is likely that Angolan children, if surveyed, would tell much the same stories as did the 504 children interviewed during a 1989 to 1990 study in Mozambique:

- 77 percent witnessed killings;

- 37 percent witnessed family members killed;

Martinho

Martinho Munikongo, 10, comes from Huambo. He lives in the Kikalanga home for children, an orphanage in Luanda. He used to live in Kapango, a shantytown on the outskirts of Huambo, where he was in first grade at the local primary school.

One day he went fishing in the River Kulimar outside the city with an older friend to try and bring home fish for his mother and the rest of the family. When he returned it was dark and guerrillas had entered the neighbourhood. They had burned many houses, including his own.

Martinho saw the burned house. He recalls: "My mother died, my father died, and my older brothers all died."

Asked if he saw his dead parents and brothers, he answers: "Yes."

And how did you feel? Were you afraid? "Yes."

What happened then? "I went to my friend's house. His mother gave me some food and I stayed there."

Martinho also recounts that the guerrillas took his friend's father into the bush and killed him.

Did you see your friend's father, dead, in the bush? "Yes."

Martinho says that he cried a lot at the time and that he was unable to sleep. Asked why, he answers: "I think about my mum."

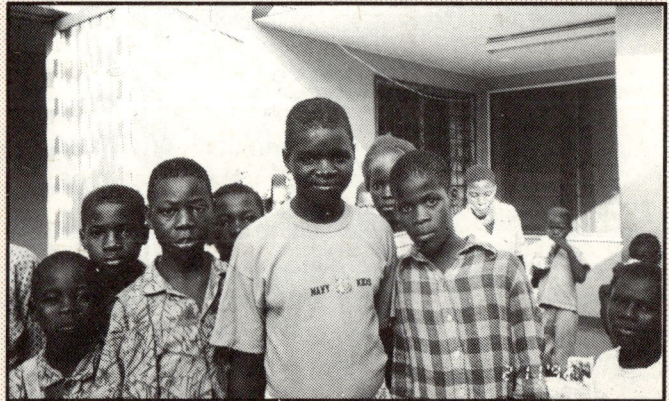

Photo 2.1: *Martinho (tallest boy in middle)*

- 88 percent witnessed physical abuse and/or torture;

- 51 percent were physically abused or tortured;

- 7 percent suffered permanent physical injury;

- 16 percent of girls admitted to being raped;

- 64 percent were abducted from their families;

- 75 percent of the abductees served as porters;

- 28 percent of the abductees trained for combat.[18]

The War-Injured

Monuments to war veterans in public squares in Europe and North America are usually of green, weathered bronze and set on pedestals with glowing tributes to people's heroism.

Angola's are at eye level and alive, on crutches, with a green army pant-leg flapping where a foot used to be.

Many tens of thousands lost limbs in Angola's war. Current estimates range from 40,000 up to 70,000 amputees. Statistically, the right lower leg has been the most common amputation, the Claymore anti-personnel mine its most common cause.

In Kuando Kubango Province, UNITA had established by 1989 a special Department for War Wounded. It was operating at least three units for war amputees. One of these was said to produce 20 artificial legs per month.[20]

Photo 2.2: *War victims at a social service centre, Lubango, Huila province.*

The International Committee of the Red Cross (ICRC) founded an orthopedic centre at Huambo in 1979, and later a similar centre at Kuito in Bie Province. In the years up to 1992, the centres made and fitted 11,000 artificial limbs. At Huambo, a mainly Angolan staff produced about 140 false legs every month, made to measure for landmine victims, who also received basic physio-therapy.

One 23-year-old woman treated there, nine years after losing a leg to a mine, was asked if her boyfriend still wanted to marry her. The reply was positive: "He is very dear," she beamed.[21]

Because so many of the victims of mines were so young, their artificial limbs will have to be repaired and replaced many times in their lifetimes. Angola's health care system will have to keep tens of thousands of people on their feet until the middle of the next century.

Civilian war amputees face a bleak future economically. The ICRC estimates that only 10 percent of those fitted with artificial limbs could, in the mid-1980s, find gainful employment in the formal sector. Another 15 percent returned to farming, while the rest remain dependent on their families and communities.[22]

Angolan war victims have let it be known that they will not be forgotten, either. Injured army veterans have begun to organize. Their persistent, and sometimes rowdy demonstrations drew public notice and sympathy. At times their anger and desperation spilled over into violence, such as

Arminda' s Story

In 1986, Arminda Antonio, 26, mother of four, of Kwanza-Sul province, lost her leg below the knee:

"It was a mine. I was going to the field. From my house...in the morning at six o'clock. I was alone with my baby Nelito on my back. I put my foot down...didn't see anything. The mine was well-hidden under the sand...the left foot down...It exploded. An enormous noise! I don't know how, but luckily nothing, nothing happened to my baby.

"My husband went to the field and found me crying and covered with blood. He also wept. He went to get his brother and the two of them carried me on their shoulders to the hospital. I stayed there two months. My mother took care of my children. Since then I've had to jump around on only one foot."

In 1991, Arminda became one of the fortunate ones to be fitted with an artificial leg at one of Angola's three main prosthetic centres, Neves Bedinha, established in 1988 in Luanda. In 1990, 742 amputees — half soldiers, half civilians — were fitted with prostheses there. Causes: 90 percent war-related, mainly explosive mines.[19]

in September, 1991, when a government army commander was murdered by a group of war-injured caught in the act of pilfering foodstuffs from an army warehouse in Lubango.[23]

The war victimized Angolans terribly, and, as later chapters will show, it goes on victimizing them. The war taught people many things, including the importance of relying on their own strengths, collectively and singly. The next chapter tells about Angolans who refused to become permanent victims.

The Suffering of War Veterans

The home for crippled war veterans in the southern city of Lubango is an old broken-down house. In it live 68 wounded veterans of FAPLA, the government army. Most are between 20 and 35. Some are blind and mute, many are missing one or both legs.

Others suffer from war traumas, or psychological problems from being cast off by society. This feeling of rejection has grown since peace came and the announcement of special measures for "normal" soldiers. Some are confounded by sudden ideological shifts — what they had fought against for so long now seems wholly acceptable.

Joao Pedro, who lost a leg, tells how he feels.

"Our government has to resolve our case before the elections, for if it's not resolved before then, we'll have no more power.

"This is no house in which to live. A number have to sleep on the cold floor. The roof leaks. We fought in the war, we lost our legs, and now we're let down. We would like better living conditions before the elections."We don't have crutches. Those should be bought. We don't have any hand-crank wheelchairs. Now that the war's over we're just old rubbish. A tin of milk with the milk poured out — you can throw that tin away. The crippled in the street also have no crutches, no wheelchairs. That should be taken care of.

"When there was war, we weren't treated as rubbish. We were still the combatants then, those who fought for the people. On the street, you still got respect. But now that the war's over, nobody's looking up to the crippled veterans.

"When we left home, from our mother's house, we left without hesitation to fight for our country. And now we sit here, with nothing. Some of the wounded veterans manage to go home, to their mothers' houses. In my case that's not possible. Why doesn't the government provide means to support our families?

"Those who made war now can't resolve these things — what the war ruined, those who lost their legs or arms or eyes. Here they can only make war, and once that's over, the wounded veterans are left on their own...

"The scar on my face? Yes, that was from Moxico in January 1985, during a battle. They came, and we tried to hit back. It was terrible what they did. But nowadays we're brothers, at least if they don't threaten us. On the battlefield it's different."

Another veteran adds:

"In those 16 years everything was destroyed. And nowadays there's peace, except for the fact that Angola is a rich country. Rich for the others, but for those who stood at the front it's not rich."

3

Survival Strategies: How Angolans Got Through the War

"**O**n 20 February 1991 there was a massacre at our orphanage. We slept in the bush while the attackers stayed in Londuimbali. We couldn't go back. So, the 66 orphanage children and I walked through the bush. It's 27 kilometres to Alto Hama. We talked to some *sobas* who offered us food. We slept there, and stayed for four days. Then a military convoy taking food to Bailundo agreed to give us a ride to Huambo. But on the road we suffered another attack. Two soldiers died. The vehicles were burned. We stayed there until another group of soldiers brought us to Huambo. There we occupied an old orphanage."

This story told by Abilio Chivasa, former director of the Londuimbali orphanage, is one of unusual courage. It is but one small reflection of the everyday survival tactics that hundreds of thousands of Angolans used to survive the war: flight from danger, use of whatever formal help was available, reliance on traditional bonds of solidarity and an iron will to live.

Wealthier Angolans had comparatively little trouble getting through the war. Most of them avoided military service. An unknown number — perhaps as many as 20,000 — took up residence in Europe, North America and Brazil.[1] Some got protected jobs in the state apparatus.

But poorer Angolans have known nothing but war all their lives, continually, and at first hand.[2] Angolan authorities, local and international charities and foreign governments did what they could to help. But their efforts were as nothing, compared with what Angolans managed to do for themselves. Most had no other choice but to rely on their own wits, connections, and meagre material resources.

Flight

Up to 1.5 million Angolans, or one in six or seven people at any given time, were forced to move from their homes during the 16 years of war. Usually they had to pack their small belongings and move unexpectedly and quickly. These movements came in waves as the war ebbed and flowed.

During the 1975-76 fighting, perhaps a million people were uprooted. Many made their way to the cities, others to neighbouring Zaire and Zambia. Still others went into the bush with UNITA.

Figure 1.1 in Chapter One shows the main lines of movement over the years. Figure 1.2 shows the number of Angolans recorded as displaced in the years 1980, 1985 and 1991. A full account of population movements would not show single displacements, but repeated shifts. If conditions worsened in one location, then a family would move on to try its luck with kinfolk in another town.

Protecting Food Supplies

How to get enough to eat? The issue preoccupied many minds. Year after year, officials estimated that supplies of food (national production plus imports) fell far short of Angola's requirements.

Maize and rice farmers radically reduced the amount of land in use. In the maize-growing province of Huila, for example, total cultivation had shrunk by about 20 percent from pre-war levels. Anti-personnel mines along footpaths, shortages of labour, exhaustion of soils, collapse of trade networks supplying farmers with oxen to pull their plows, poor market incentives, lack of farm-to-market transport and the risk of pillage and theft all combined to depress maize-growing. (See Figure 3.1.)

Yet, despite serious hunger at certain moments among specific groups (especially the displaced), Angola never became like some parts of Sudan or Ethiopia, a land of walking skeletons.

The very poor in Angola have always known hunger, especially when they lost land, livestock or income at the hands of settlers; or when their crops and pastures perished during periodic droughts. After such disasters it would take at least a season to regain some food security.

The war pushed many more small farmers into the category of the very poor, keeping them there for years.

Few, however, were completely vulnerable. That is because Angolan farmers possess some of Africa's most sophisticated indigenous farming systems. The animal-drawn plough, intercropping and intricate irrigation techniques are widely used. Against natural hazards farmers have built up vast reserves of knowledge to get through bad times.

Farmers' defences against the devastations of war were weaker, but not negligible:[4]

- Where surrounding land was spiked with mines, or belonged to others, the best option was to cultivate available ground more intensively. The tiny gardens, some no bigger than a bedsheet, in most Angolan cities and towns bore witness to this economy of soil use.

- Maize is a favoured crop, but not nearly as resistant as the Angolan small grains which can cope with dry soils and poor rainfall. These small grains — chiefly millet and sorghum — were in widespread use in central Angola during the war. People knew their obvious advantages, despite the risks of birds and the extra work needed to de-hull the grains before they could be eaten.

- The hardy cassava advanced southwards during the war years. A cassava stem planted even in mediocre soils would yield a plump tuber after 18 months, drought or no drought. People with little experience of cassava — and some disdain for it — learned to appreciate its

Figure 3.1: *Maize Seed Input Gap*

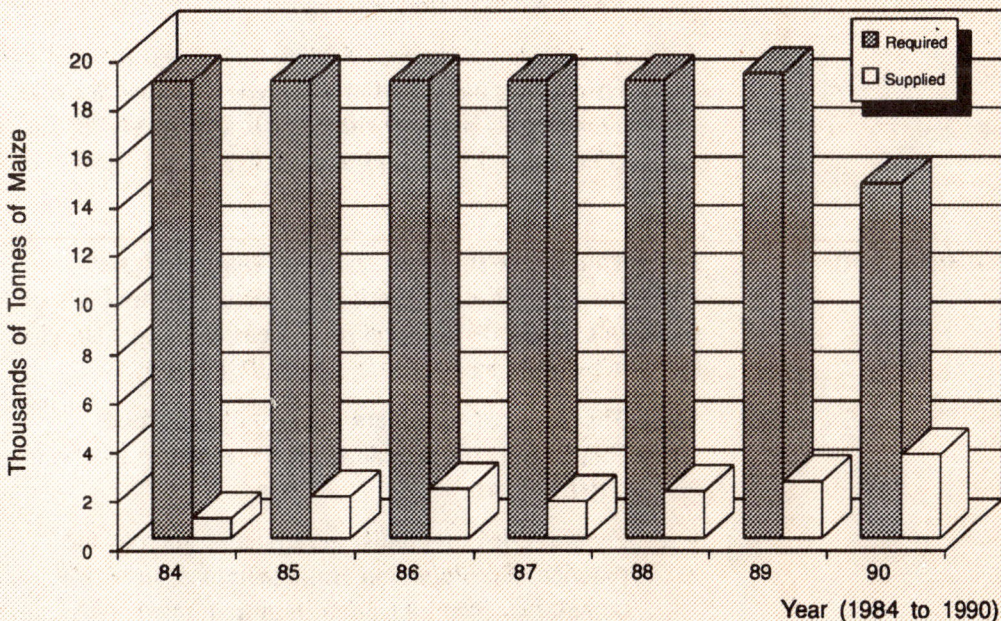

qualities. Cassava growing has taken up more crop land than it did before 1975, and national output is well above pre-war levels. And it continues its advance: government estimates for 1992 suggest an expansion of 20 percent in land use devoted to cassava since 1990.

- The sweet potato likewise gained popularity, providing both calories and nutrients. It, too, spread southward into the central highlands. Like the cassava, it requires only modest weeding. Unlike the cassava, preparation for eating was easy and quick.

- Especially in the warm valleys of central and north-western zones, people took care to plant extra banana trees. For many, the banana became an important secondary source of calories.

- Where the terrain was safe, men took up their fathers' and grandfathers' hunting tradition. Everything from antelope to field mice was fair game.

- Fishing in local streams and lagoons, usually a task for women using traditional woven reed traps, became a serious activity for all family members.

- After harvesting, grains and other crops had to be hidden against the likely raids of pillaging soldiers. But this did not always work. A *soba* from N'harea in Bie province told an inquiring journalist after the war: "It did not matter where we hid our food or other things, because the guerrillas are our own sons and they know where we keep things."

- To sustain themselves through to the next harvest, most farmers carefully husbanded seeds from the last one. This genetic pillar of rural life is now receiving the attention and importance it merits.

Procuring Food

Not even the best-endowed farmer is completely self-sufficient. And those without land, including hundreds of thousands of displaced in the rural areas and city shantytowns, had to find food by whatever means they could:

- They worked for others in exchange for food. Displaced people became the "new" cheap labour for other farmers.

- People relied on mutual aid systems, such as the practice of *onduluca* in Huila province, in which community members pitch in to help plant, weed, and harvest each others' crops.[5] In Huambo and Malanje provinces such practices have disappeared, but community solidarity during death and mourning is common.

Urban dwellers had better access to whatever food sources were available, but rural people also took advantage of relief through charities and state food

Our Own Seeds are Better

War and isolation forced local farmers back to basics. Chemical fertilizers, hybrid seeds and other modern, imported inputs which salesmen and extension agents of the colonial era had promoted were no longer available. To use one's own seeds was a step backward, it seemed; the yields were lower. But in times of stress, they proved more resistant.

Liz Matos, a member of the Department of Biology of the

Photo 3.1: *Children in Catholic Church feeding programme in Huambo*

Science Faculty at the National University in Luanda, is clear about the advantages of local seed varieties: "Our seeds are better, more resistant. We need to take advantage of what they have to offer."

She and colleagues launched an experimental programme in the southern provinces of Huila and Namibe. "We have a worthwhile experiment, developed with about 30 small farmers, to whom we distributed sacks of seed and forms. They've carried the work out very well, and we've had a lot of cooperation from them."

The collection of local seed varieties complements similar work in other southern African countries, centring chiefly on crops for semi-arid conditions with no irrigation. These are mainly sorghum and millet, which are basic to the diets of people living there. The aim is to select the best from among the local seeds and preserve and multiply the germplasm (the genetic heart of the seed) in them.

There is rising concern that such genetic resources may die out in the region — or even be "expropriated" through biotechnology patents by transnational seed corporations — as the juggernaut of "modernization" in farming rolls on. Such trends have caused farmers to doubt their own genetic resources and their own knowledge.

The results of such "modernization" can be disastrous. In southern Angola in 1987 there was a major effort to promote hybrid maize. Many farmers accepted the seeds in good faith, expecting that under the right conditions — especially sufficient rainfall — they would yield much more per hectare than indigenous seeds.

But in 1988-89, a terrible drought afflicted the area. The "right conditions" were out of farmers' control. The "modern" hybrid maize died. Many had not planted their own varieties because they had believed in the "experts". Many people suffered hunger in the south of Angola that year.

The war helped show that the way to the future was through the past, through local seeds and local know-how.

relief programmes. Such aid was not insignificant, especially for people officially classified as "displaced". But for those few rural Angolans who had access to it, food aid merely supplemented their diet a few weeks in a year. Most of the time it was simply not available.[6]

- Food first, then ethics: For many Angolans beset by hunger, to steal food was to survive. The main targets were fields, gardens, livestock pens and corrals, or shops, delivery trucks and warehouses. One of the great disincentives to farming in urban areas has been the high risk of loss to thieves — usually meaning other hungry people.

- Finally, most Angolans stretched what reserves they had by simply going hungry.

The whip of hunger not only drove people back to basics in producing and finding food. It also obliged them to take up new trades. Resourcefulness, ingenuity, and plain cunning have flourished as never before. So, too, has simple desperation. As a result, Anogolans have taken up various lines of work to survive.

Trade

Since the 1700s, Angolans have been among the most active long-distance traders. The people of the highlands in the 1800s became, for most of south-central Africa, "the greatest purveyors of slaves, ivory, and wax for the harbours on the coast."[7] The Portuguese colonizers tried to suppress Angolan merchants, but never managed to snuff out their entrepreneurial spirit. With the end of colonialism, trading re-emerged with great energy.

How many worked full-time as traders? One estimate was about 300,000 persons active in "parallel markets" in 1990, representing seven percent of the economically active population.[8] The majority were women.

But at one time or another, *most* Angolans took part in the business of buying cheap at one time and place and selling dear in another. It has been estimated that about a third of every working person's productive time was devoted to some kind of petty business transaction, mainly to obtain food.

At one time or another during the war years, almost every household in Angola used trade as one of its key survival strategies.

Services

Some people who traded for survival had to go a step further. Traditional cattle-keepers in Angola's livestock-rich southern scrub and grasslands — men who looked on commerce with suspicion, if not contempt — are now selling and butchering their cows at the roadside. The shift in vocation from aloof pastoralist to price-wise merchant-butcher differs only in degree from the flexibility that tens of thousands of others have shown to survive.

Tinker, Tailor

Tinsmiths and blacksmiths quickly emerged in great numbers to make and repair cooking pots and farm tools. As second-hand clothes began trickling into rural trading circuits, tailors soon arrived to repair or adjust the apparel. Not only Angolans, but also itinerant tailor-merchants from Zaire and Senegal made money in this market.

With the breakdown of motorized transport, many people served as porters or transporters using animal or human-powered vehicles.

The Micro-Enterprise

In the towns and cities the range of services grew wider and more specialized. Men took up jobs as mini-bus drivers and fare-collectors. They began hammering and soldering back into shape the autos battered in collisions. Or, they merely began to wash cars.

Those with means to acquire a tanker truck used it to collect untreated water from a nearby river and sell it by the litre in shantytowns.

Women began looking after the children of others, taking in their laundry and cleaning their houses. They plaited others' hair — the latest styles require a day's work. And some worked as prostitutes.

Re-cycling, always common in Africa, became more intense as men and women collected every bit of scrap paper and metal that could be recycled or used in some enterprise.

Those with a bit more capital made wedding cakes in backyard bakeries.

Traditional medical services became more of a business, and more traditional healers entered it. Before the 1980s, traditional healers would accept payments according to patients' ability to pay. Some were treated free. War and

Survival: From Teacher to Goat Trader — and Back

Like many others, Filipe Ngonda Makengo survived the war by leaving familiar home ground and eagerly seizing whatever chances that came along.

Born in 1951 in a traditional farming family in the northern province of Uige, Makengo knew war from an early age. His father died as a resistance fighter of the UPA (Union of the People of Angola) at the beginning of the anti-colonial war in 1961. In that year Portuguese settlers killed at least 20,000 Angolans in an orgy of blood-letting. That war forced the family, with most other villagers, to flee into the bush. They lived there for two years, moving from hiding-place to hiding-place to avoid spotter planes and ground troops.

But one day a Portuguese patrol captured Makengo and three other boys, bathing in a river. It was a lesson in anti-insurgency "hearts-and-minds" tactics. After an interrogation, the soldiers sent the boys back to their parents with food, clothing and advice to everyone in hiding: come out and return to your village, for the war is over.

The family eventually did so. Makengo was able to finish primary schooling, and a short teacher training course. He began teaching primary school in his home village in 1969 until 1975, when the major upheavals began.

Moving to Songo, a place of greater security, he continued teaching until 1983, when guerrillas arrived and destroyed the village, including the school. With life deteriorating around him almost daily, Makengo finally decided to start a new life in Luanda. Through his extended family networks he made his way at first to the neighbourhood called Petrangol, and later the mainly Kikongo-speaking area called Palanca.

He had no difficulty finding work as a teacher in a profession which had lost its prestige since the colonial era. It was a fallback, not a promotion, to become a "professor" in Luanda. A primary school teacher's salary would keep one alive for barely 10 days per month. Some of his students ate better, and looked healthier, than he did. Their parents sympathized, and would send Makengo small gifts; but during exam period they would ask him to give their children a pass mark.

With these pressures and the hopelessly inadequate salary, he decided to quit. Black marketeering was not ideal work, but there was no choice if he and his family were to survive.

So he got into the goat trade. It all started when his wife's brother sent a radio/cassette player from West Germany, where he'd fled to avoid the war. They sold the device immediately, giving them a chunk of capital, the likes of which they'd never seen before.

From Parque, one of Luanda's market areas where up-country vehicles come and go, Makengo began his journeys to Sumbe, 400 kilometres to the south. There he would buy half a dozen goats for somewhere between 12,000 and 15,000 kwanzas each — about US$6 to US$7. Since goats sold in Luanda for 25,000 to 40,000 kwanzas according to size, and the truckers charged only 2,500-a head, this was more lucrative than teaching school.

Added to these returns was his wife's income from selling small items in an open market called "Help the Husband". Soon the family began eating better, buying new clothes, and planning to buy some furniture.

It was not to be. Inflation caught up with the goat trade, and profit margins dropped. Then, in 1991 the government raised public service salaries, including those of teachers. Makengo re-applied for his old work and today he is once again teaching primary school, prestige or no prestige.

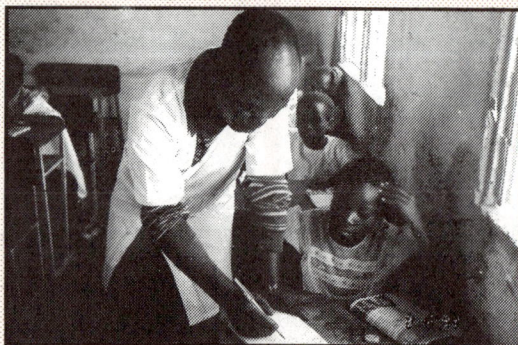

Photo 3.2: *Filipe Ngonda Makengo as teacher*

economic pressures changed all that as healers began asking for cash payment: 35,000 kwanzas (US$18) to treat mental illness. Dealing with sterility cost at least 50,000 kwanza (US$25).

Odd-Jobbing

Despite advantages it offered in access to subsidized goods, the return to formal employment steadily diminished during the war years which meant that many people worked in both the formal (registered) *and* informal (unregistered) sectors. They juggled both by taking after-hours work, or simply neglecting their formal jobs. Some gladly shifted completely to the informal because the pay was so much better. Among them are often the better-schooled. One young man, after training as a parts clerk and getting a good job in the warehouse of a Swedish truck outlet in Luanda, left after two years for the more lucrative trade in luxury items.

Some state schools and health units, for example, provided such abysmal working conditions that teachers and nurses abandoned them to give private lessons or health services in their homes for payment.

Direct Production

Those who put their efforts into direct production were the greatest risk-takers.

Growing maize and beans for the market meant coping with the risk of uncertain rainfall and other natural hazards. It also meant getting by with collapsed commercial networks and unreliable transport to obtain inputs or get goods to market. For this reason, the most successful were market gardeners and fishermen and women close to major towns and cities.

Greenbelt farmers

Urban agriculture and animal husbandry became a growth industry during the war, with an estimated 138,000 persons (three-quarters of them women) at work on peri-urban plots.[10] Irrigating these gardens and caring for pigs, goats and chickens put further pressure on already over-taxed urban water supply systems, and may have accounted for water losses (50 per cent in the case of Luanda) between pumping stations and city taps.[11]

Irrigate, Irrigate

A recent study exposed a little-known, but formidable technology used in rural survival strategies. It concerns indigenous systems of water management, especially the use of land in and near moist valley bottoms or *olonacas*. Surveys of farms in the 1960s suggested that three out of five farmers (most of them in the central highlands) practiced some form of small-scale irrigation based on these moist lands. Perhaps to the surprise of plantation bosses, this micro-irrigation accounted for 80 per cent of all irrigated land in Angola.[12] With the war limiting access to rain fed fields, Angolan farmers — the majority of them women — expanded

Scooting for Cargo

With most bridges blown up, dirt roads mined and trucks and pickups easy targets for ambushes, the people of Kwanza Sul faced slow starvation midway through the 1980s. Many perished, especially if they were on the run, seeking refuge from even more desperate circumstances.

Farmers were producing grain and other foods, and merchants were ready to buy. Yet, only the brave or the foolhardy took what few motor vehicles there were onto inland roads, to span the gap between supply and demand.

In typical Angolan fashion, ingenuity stepped into the gap. Somewhere, someone came up with an answer. Perhaps recalling a childhood plaything, he or she made a scooter entirely out of wood, loaded it with bags of produce, and began hauling cargo from point A to B. The technology spread. Soon tons of goods began to move in Kwanza Sul — and beyond.

Whole fleets of scooters — *trotinetas* — were manufactured in backyards. Routes and regular clients were established. Repair depots sprang up along major routes to handle breakdowns: "Bearings burned out sir? We've got just the spare part you need!"

Transit police at towns such as Gabela sometimes had to cope with 30 or 40 scooters arriving at once, creating traffic jams.

Some scooters could handle up to four sacks of maize, meaning perhaps 200 kilogrammes of cargo. Routes of 70 to 100 kilometres were not uncommon for some carriers, who could ask as much as 10,000 kwanzas (US$5) in freight charges, depending on distance.

The technology was wholly Angolan. No donor or well-meaning do-gooder parachuted the thing in as part of a project. No appropriate technology enthusiast arrived to deliver it to a reluctant and bewildered "target group". The full story of the wartime *trotineta* in Angola has yet to be told, but when it is, the protagonists will doubtless be only "simple" Angolans.

Photo 3.3: *Trotinetas, the new means of cargo transport*

and intensified their use of the irrigated *olonacas* to feed their families.

Tending the Herds

Vietnam-style warfare with South African helicopter gunships, tank columns and search-and-destroy platoons swept through the southern provinces of Cunene and Huila many times beginning in late 1975. Nevertheless, the semi-nomadic pastoralists living there have survived, and their herds of

---

Fishmonger

"I come here to Zambeca for two or three weeks to buy fish," says Arlinda, the fishmonger. "I go back to Luanda to sell the fish in different markets. After two or three weeks I come back to the village for more fish. That's my work."

Arlinda is typical of many traders who regularly travel the 100 or so kilometres between Luanda and Cassoneca, an area near the Kwanza river southeast of the nation's capital. Zambeca is one of 21 small villages in the area. Arlinda, the daughter of a Cassoneca resident, moved to Luanda years ago to work in the markets.

She is one of an estimated 300,000 Angolans working in "parallel" circuits of exchange. These farmers, fishing people and artisans make up three-quarters of the workforce categorized as the "informal" sector, where women form the majority.

Zambeca is like many inland fishing villages whose residents fish and tend their gardens to feed themselves and, at the same time, actively sell or trade any surpluses for other goods and services. As well as maize, cassava, sweet potatoes, beans, tomatoes and other vegetables, Zambeca's families catch *bagre* (cat-fish) and *cacuso* in one of the lagoons of the Kwanza River.

Traditionally, men fish and women cure and sell the catches. Most fish is sun-dried, smoked or salted. Because of the war and poor transport, little salt reached northern Angola from the south coast where production exceeds demand, and a lot of fish spoils.

With its 2,000 square kilometres of rivers and lagoons, Angola has an enormous natural base for inland fishing. At least 5,000 Angolans fish for a living, using both local and imported means. The war and breakdown of supply lines has brought back indigenous devices, such as fish traps developed and used in Angola for centuries. Once again, local know-how, rather than foreign relief, has helped most people survive.

Angola's inland waters, carry a potential yield of up to 113,000 tonnes of fish per year, yet only a fraction of this is pulled ashore.[9]

"Most fish sellers," continues Arlinda, "return to the same village each time. I always come to Zambeca because my sister is married to a fisherman here. I pay transport to come here by truck. To go back to Luanda, I carry the fish in a big sack for which I also have to pay transport."

Arlinda does well, but she is small fry in the business. "There are some extremely rich women fishmongers who employ other women to sell their fish," says Dan Rosengren, Swedish anthropologist and socio-economist. "These employees are usually paid in kind with fish. On the Ilha [the small island just off Luanda], fishermen talk about one of the really rich women fish sellers, a Cape Verdean married to a local carpenter. She employs other women to cure and sell her fish. She herself never appears on the market, but has a regular set of customers who buy her fish."

cattle and goats have grown. Southern Angola's cattle now number more than 3.5 million head, having been estimated at 2.7 million in 1971. (Many cattle perished during the 1975-76 war in the south, and the 1988-89 drought.)

A survey of food security among people living in the harsh, semi-desert rangelands of Cunene showed that, even months after a bad drought, rates of malnutrition were low and the average granary well-stocked.[13] The exceptions were, as usual, those recently displaced by war. The people of Cunene clearly practice some sound strategies of survival.

Furnishing Fuelwood

Whoever cooks without gas or kerosene must rely on firewood and charcoal. Woodfuels account for about 92 percent of all Angola's domestic energy consumption.[14] In villages and shantytowns, the task of fetching fuelwood falls to women and children as part of their household chores. But for most urban households, and for hospitals, schools, and military barracks it is a commercial matter. Provision of fuelwood and charcoal continue to grow as businesses. Around the city of Namibe, the trade tripled in volume between 1974 and 1986. Around Luanda, charcoal-making was outlawed in 1983, forcing it underground, and pushing up prices. It has become a lucrative business, especially for those with trucks.[15] Of course, this had consequences for the peri-urban environment (See Chapter Four).

Photo 3.4: *A granary in Huila province.*

Blacksmithing

Recorded supplies of farm tools — hoes, machetes, plows and plow parts — continuously fell short of farmers' needs in the post-independence period. (See Figure 3.2.) A 1988 survey in rural areas of Huila showed that crop farmers and pastoralists put the lack of tools high on their list of major problems.[16] This also became a national problem because it helped depress farm output, lower living standards, and alienate farmers from Luanda.

But rural people didn't stand by waiting for someone else to solve their problems. Among them, blacksmiths emerged in most farming regions to help fill the tool gap. Scrap steel is their raw material. A 1989 report suggested that as many as 2,500 blacksmiths, most of them part-time farmers, were at work in the southern provinces alone. They supplied farmers and herdsmen with hoes, knives, machetes and repair services cheaply and efficiently, adapting their work to local requirements.[17]

Brick-making and Building

Invisible to those who chronicle the state-supervised construction and building materials industries, but striking to the eye of anyone visiting the edges of Angola's towns and cities, is the scale and dynamism of brickmaking and construction by local artisans. In 1989, an estimated 29 billion kwanzas (US$15 million) in the parallel market went toward construction in Luanda alone. That amount was more

Photo 3.5:
Blacksmiths at work in deslocados camp in Caluquembe, Huila province.

than three times the total kwanza value of all officially-recorded construction activities in Angola in that year.[18]

Construction provided about eight per cent of informal employment in Luanda in 1990, after trade and tailoring, according to an important survey on poverty and survival in Luanda.[19] In other places the proportion could be much higher.

Self-Reliance

The list of activities is unusually long, even in African terms. Yet it could be extended with more examples, from footwear-makers to diamond-smugglers.

Following a violent break with the colonial order — whose main legacy was the shallowest possible pool of skilled people — war and economic disorder shattered the formal, controllable systems of economic life. Most of what was once officially monitored and exploited, such as small-scale farming, shrank in size. Surpluses for sale went underground and new, dynamic activities appeared to fill the vacuum. In this sense the people's economy of wartime Angola was a noteworthy case of what has been happening elsewhere in Africa. The failures of the formal economy to satisfy basic

Figure 3.2: *Farm Hoes Input Gap*

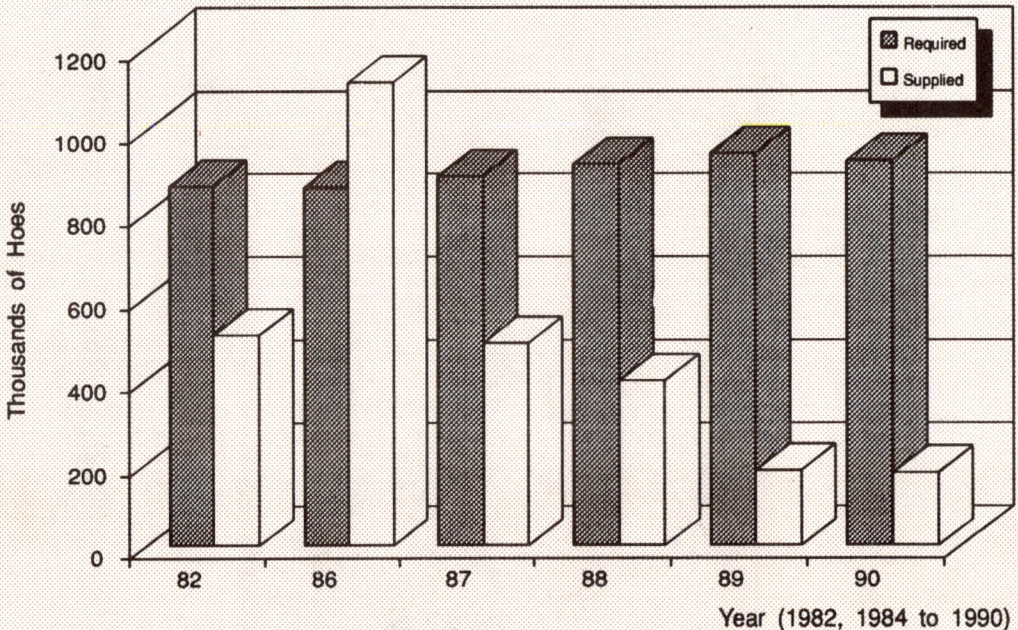

needs even in the peaceful conditions prevailing elsewhere in Africa have brought forward local solutions.[20]

But a goods famine continued. Most forms of production declined. The growth area was in circulation and speculation — trade, transport, money-changing, hoarding and renting out rooms. Money was to be made faster and with fewer risks in those activities, not in production.

For the majority, the motto became "look out for yourself". Solutions for oneself and one's personal network came first. Solutions for the public at large became nobody's business.

Angolan men and women survived, often with ingenious strategies, but many did not as desperation grew.

4

The Cost of War: Physical and Environmental

In early 1987, a mortar attack partially demolished the Angolan Institute of Veterinary Research outside Huambo. As the Institute was about to manufacture millions of doses of vaccine, the attack crippled an important effort to combat three deadly diseases affecting the country's cattle.

The destruction pushed back an innoculation programme, further exposing livestock to infectious diseases, including anthrax, which also kills people. It meant a further drain on scarce foreign exchange, since vaccines then had to be imported. It also meant loss of contact with herdsmen, anxious to see their livestock innoculated.

The episode illustrates the repercussions of war damage on Angolan life. The aftershocks — economic, political and cultural — were many. Yet, the cause was just one, rather small, destructive event. There have been thousands of such events, and Angola is still paying the price.

As with similar wars of the late 20th century, the economy was the target. Destruction or paralysis of whatever the economy needed to work and grow, were everyday events in Angola's war.

Field and Farm

Often forgotten among the sagas of oil-tank sabotage and dockside destruction is the impact of war on the farm lands.

Almost nine million hectares (about seven percent of Angola's 1.2 million square kilometres) were classified as farm land before the war. About half this land supported 700,000 "traditional" farms. The other half consisted of over 6,000 holdings as plantations and "commercial" farms. Both "commercial" and "traditional" farmers used only part of their lands, a large fraction was usually kept fallow.[1]

Fifteen years into the war, government data for 1989 and 1990 suggested that only 1.2 million hectares were being cultivated, only a quarter of that in use 20 years earlier — and this for a rural population one million persons larger.[2]

Yet other official data do not suggest quite such radical shrinkage. On the contrary, they show expansion of fields devoted to millet and sorghum, cassava, and especially sweet potato in the period 1986 to 1990. Those are crops in which state marketing authorities took little interest, but hungry farmers seeking drought- and pillage-resistant crops evidently took a different view.

Whatever the details of crop substitution, the war nonetheless forced farmers to stop using much of their land. The many reports, confirmed by aerial photos, of abandoned villages and farmlands cannot be denied. The effect was uneven: some farmers quit their fields completely while others let more land lie fallow for longer periods. Non-food cash crops were the first to be abandoned. Farmers ripped up coffee bushes and planted cassava instead. Areas which were once modestly prosperous became de-populated bushlands.

Cattle were hard hit, as the World Bank says in a 1991 report:

"Cattle-raising in southern Angola is becoming increasingly difficult. South African troops have systematically destroyed the water spots (artesian wells, small dams and water pools), most of which are now unusable. In consequence of the water problem, security and policy conditions, several areas where cattle were previously raised are now almost deserted."[3]

Photo 4.1: *War damage from artillery fire at Caluquembe, Huila province.*

Larger-scale farming also suffered. No inventory has been made of damage to farm buildings, pumps, tractors and irrigation channels. But the vast abandoned and overgrown fields where sisal, cotton, sugar and coffee once grew testify to the violent rupture with the settler order, and to the 16 years of war that followed.

Some of these farms, especially in the well-watered highlands, may be off-limits for years. As Chapter Six explains, they are saturated with mines.

Processing Primary Products

The war choked off supplies of raw materials to most agrarian-based industries in Angola. Especially hard hit were those relying on the produce of small farmers and livestock keepers — grain mills, textile plants, dairies, meat and hide plants, oil presses and coffee processors.

Some closed altogether. But most were kept running, usually at less than a third of capacity, on imported raw materials paid for in hard currency. They soon lost any economic justification they may have had. Nevertheless, pride and bureaucratic imperatives often won the day: one factory went right on producing ornamental candles, several others manufactured cookies. One of the war's negative economic impacts was the excessive drain on precious foreign exchange.

Among the more dramatic direct losses to such industries were the aerial bombardment of a woodworking plant in the industrial zone of Lubango in September 1979, in which 26 workers were killed, and the destruction of a pulp and paper mill at Alto Catumbela, Benguela province in March 1983.

The war caused the loss of many small-town grain mills and oil presses so important to small farmers, especially women. Some were destroyed by bombs and mortars. By cutting off flows of raw material, spare parts, lubricants, energy, and managerial know-how, the war did its destructive work just as effectively by slow strangulation.

Transportation and Distribution Infrastructure

Road and rail transport, and their linked systems of ports and warehouses, were prime targets during the war. But so, too, were more modest means of transportation.

Pathways

Carrying goods on the head — the most basic kind of cargo transport for Angolans in daily life — did not escape the attention of military tacticians. Mines or booby traps laid along pathways claimed thousands of victims, and continue to claim them, as described in Chapter Six. They effectively achieved their main aim, which was to deny people access to fields and pastures, schools and clinics, fuelwood and building materials, water and social contact.

Roads

The war slowed traffic to a dangerous crawl, and in many areas stopped road movement altogether. Truck drivers, who faced ambushes and landmines, stand high on the list of unsung heroes of the war years.

According to the World Bank, 60 percent of the 7,500 kilometres of asphalted roads needed rehabilitation or reconstruction by 1987. The 1,500 kilometres of gravel roads were also in deplorable shape. Since then, most road surfaces have deteriorated further, and some have crumbled completely.

The World Bank also says that "war conditions are largely responsible for driving up real tonne-per-kilometre rates by 300 percent (and over 420 percent when the impact of poor highway maintenance is estimated)." Poor roads mean shorter vehicle life. Few German-made IFA trucks survived longer than six months under "normal" conditions.

Slower speeds also raised costs. "Trips that were accomplished in a week (e.g., Luanda-Andrada-Luanda) prior to guerilla activities now take a month on average and have been as long as 53 days, principally because of convoy operations," says a World Bank report.[4]

All this helped to break down vital circuits of trade. (See Box below.)

Hunger in the Cities

"Right now the people of Buengas are going hundreds of kilometres on foot, suffering a lot to fetch salt, fish and other products."

A government official of Uige Province sums up the consequences of road damage in the richest farming zones of his province. Thousands of tonnes of cassava and rice were said to be rotting in various parts of Uige in early 1992 because the merchants' trucks could not get through; the roads are just too potholed.

"There's no reason for so much hunger in the cities," said one observer. "If commerce could just take a little care of things, the cities will be full of food."[5]

Such costs, together with the sheer absence of transport in many zones, have driven down growth and reduced living standards.

Bridges

Few things can isolate communities more — and thus endanger food security — than blowing up bridges. In the period 1975 to 1976, about 128 bridges were destroyed, of which 79 had been repaired by 1978.[6]

Some were destroyed and repaired more than once. For example, the 812-metre bridge at Xangongo in the far south, was "put out of action in 1979, rebuilt, then destroyed again during South Africa's Operation Protea in August 1981, and then rebuilt a second time at a cost of some US$50 million".[7]

Junk

Scrap metal is one of Angola's more important products. During the war years, about 10,000 tonnes were added each year to the stock of scrap metal in the southwestern provinces alone. Overall, the country has generated about 50,000 tonnes of scrap metal a year — most of it in destroyed or abandoned cars and trucks. By 1990 as much as half a million tonnes of scrap metal may have accumulated, most of it in the vehicle graveyards of the two armed forces.

Angolan junk is described by UN experts as "rich in non-ferrous metals (aluminium, lead and copper), civil construction materials (tubes, different kinds of metal sheet, shaped metals), cars, engines, alloyed steel parts and other different equipment for second-hand utilization."

At present Angola's sixth-ranking export is metallic junk. In 1990, it earned almost US$ 6 million — far more than coffee exports. Scrap processors supplied the national steelworks with almost all its raw material.

The Angolan defence ministry's scrap metal company, which possesses most of the nation's reserves of junk, announced in March 1992 that it was to form a joint venture with a South African firm to compress and ship to South Africa tonnes of scrap metal in the years ahead.

South Africa, of course, helped to create Angola's military junk in the first place. Is it right that a South African company should now make money from it? The Angolan Minister of Defence evidently put such considerations aside when he clinched the deal in March 1992. *C'est la guerre.*

Photo 4.2: *Vehicles destroyed by mines a good source of junk*

After 1980 more than 200 bridges were destroyed, 28 of them in 1990 alone. About 300 bridges, or about one-in-10 in the country, was in need of repair or replacement at the end of the war.[6]

By late 1991 a crash programme had begun to restore the use of 50 bridges along key routes. Metal plates were laid down to span the gaps, a simple and cheap expedient (average cost: US$100,000 per bridge), but only a temporary means of opening access. Permanent repair of Angola's bridges will cost much more.

The repairs meant a dramatic release from isolation for many communities: food could come in and out, while seeds, tools, clothing and salt could reach farmers, and people could return home. Moreover, open access meant that voter registration and elections could take place in those areas. No bridges, no democracy.

Vehicles

The war and poor maintenance put many thousands of trucks and buses off the road, most of them for good. In 1974, before the war began, non-military trucks numbered 28,000, of which only 6,000 were still around in 1976. In 1987, after a massive import drive, there were about 30,000 trucks, but less than half of these were actually working. In the three southwestern provinces of Huila, Cunene and Namibe in 1987, where the state of supply routes and security were above the national average at the time, only 167 of 286 trucks (58 percent of trucks, 55 percent of capacity in tonnes) were in working condition.[9]

Direct war damage to truck fleets accounted for only part of this low rate of use. Indirect effects, including spare-part shortages and maintenance, accounted for most of it.

Bus transport was a service Angolans considered essential by the end of the colonial era. With cargo on top and passengers inside, the bus was vital to farmers, fishermen and petty traders. In 1978, more than 700 buses were on the roads.[10] By 1985 only 121 buses were actually in use, mainly in the cities, where service had virtually collapsed. By 1987 buses in Luanda carried only 13 per cent of the number of passengers carried in 1980.[11]

Rural bus service fared worse. Some especially bloody attacks on buses took place in the central provinces in 1983. By 1985 buses had virtually stopped running on rural and inter-urban routes except in the more secure zones in the south.

Desperate people switched to riding on top of trucks and their cargoes. Such private passenger solutions no doubt account for most rural mobility in the war years.

In early 1992 private entrepreneurs began putting their buses back onto the highways. A company dating from the 1950s, EVA, set up bus service between Luanda, Sumbe and Benguela and between Lubango and Cahama. It hoped to open lines to Huambo and Bie from Luanda once more buses were acquired.[12]

In the cities, beginning with Luanda, the mini-bus began making its appearance in the 1980s. (See Chapter Five).

The bicycle, the vehicle of choice in the countryside, was another victim of war. Two Angolan factories produced 36,500 bicycles in 1973 alone; five years later, they produced only a quarter of this number. Output fell even further thereafter. In 1983 about 19,000 bicycles (5,000 Angolan-made, the rest imports) were sold, meeting only a fraction of demand.

In late 1991, foreign exchange was allocated to revive bicycle production through a joint venture with an Indian company. This was Angola's first major manufacturing project based on South-South cooperation. By early 1992, some 120 bikes made from Indian kits were rolling off an assembly line every day in Luanda, with 65,000 kits having been contracted.[13] If spares, tubes and puncture repair kits also begin reaching the market, it will be a happy day for Angolans, whose mobility reached all-time lows during the war.

Rail Service

"Along the line can be seen how barbarous was the war just ended: stations completely destroyed, machines, carriages and boxcars thrown to the side of the rails are vivid testimony of the mines exploded and of the many attacks carried out."[14] This was the sight meeting a journalist on the Malanje line a few months after the peace accords.

Working from 1987 data, the World Bank states, "Destruction of at least 45 bridges and key sections of track has virtually paralyzed regional rail movement and only 20 percent of the system can be operated normally." Much more damage took place after those findings were made.

Workers on Angola's railways, one of the largest parastatal employers, suffered hundreds of casualties. On the Belgian-owned Benguela Line, alone almost 500 workers lost their lives from 1976 to 1991 as a result of thousands of acts of sabotage. Total material damage over the period 1976 to 1987 came to US$76.7 million and lost revenues for the same period to US$1.18 billion.[15] Total rail revenues in 1987 were only 12 percent of what they were in 1974.

The loss of rail service in the 1980s was a hard blow to ordinary citizens living along the three rail corridors. After 1975 Angolans began to use the trains in large numbers; by 1980 the railways carried 7.6 million passengers, two-and-a-half times that of 1973. The war broke this upward trend, which also hurt commerce, for in Angola, a travelling passenger is usually a travelling petty trader, with many kilos of goods.

Destruction and sabotage, however, curbed further growth in passenger traffic.[16] Some estimates of rehabilitation costs:

- Luanda-Malanje Line (10 bridges out): $US15 million;

- Benguela Line (75 of the 97 bridges out): US$600-plus million;

- Namibe-Matala-Cassinga line: $US33.5 million; with new rolling stock (including five new locomotives): $US41.5 million.[17]

Their economic value, and simply their importance to citizens in need of mobility, have won for the railways a high post-war priority for repair.

The Luanda-Malanje line re-opened to passenger traffic in late August, 1991, following 72 days of intensive work. On the Lobito-Huambo stretch of the Benguela line, more than 300 kilometres of track had been repaired within two months of the signing of the peace accords. This allowed trains to run, albeit slowly at 20 to 30 km per hour.[18]

The Southern African Development Coordination Conference (SADCC) has a 10-year development plan for the rehabilitation of the Lobito Corridor, including the Benguela railway, the harbour, road and sea transport, a hydroelectric dam, telecommunications, the cement factory and city water supply. Total cost of the three-phase plan, approved at a special donors' meeting in 1989, is US$530 million.

Full restoration of all rail lines, however, may not be justified economically. The issue will depend on world copper and cobalt prices affecting the Benguela line's former major users,

Zambia and Zaire. It will also depend on emphasis given trucking inside Angola.

Telecommunications

The war destroyed about 30 percent of telecommunication infrastructure for inter-city calls. Of 110 telecommunication stations and relay points in 1975, only 38 were operating in 1980. More were damaged later, resulting in the loss of half the country's transmission capacity. Direct war damage costs were US$22 million; loss of revenue was US$21 million.[19]

However, the number of telephone subscribers has more than tripled since the war began. In 1974, there were 24,501 lines;

Those Dam Repairs

Cutting off supplies of electricity and fuel was a key objective during the war, with much of the damage resulting from direct action by the South African military. Not all repair costs have been established, and in many cases revenue losses have not been calculated. Some major cases of destruction were:

Electricity:

- Lomaum hydroelectric plant, a key source of power for Benguela and Huambo provinces, was sabotaged partially in January 1983 and again, definitively, in July 1984. A programme of repair and extension got underway in 1988. Total projected cost: US$42 million.[21]

- Mabubas hydroelectric dam, 12 kilometres from Caxito in Bengo province. Rehabilitation costs estimated at US$10 million.[22]

- Kamacupa hydroelectric dam, Bie Province, sabotaged November 1990.

- Andulo hydroelectric dam, Bie Province.

- Power pylons between Cambambe and Luanda: 15 destroyed on 25 November 1984; seven destroyed on 11 December 1984. The power line Cambambe-Gabela (Kwanza Sul province) was destroyed in 1984; 10 pylons between Luanda and Mabubas destroyed in November 1990.

- Diesel generators at Kassinga Iron mines, Huila province, damaged by a South African raid, 16 May 1982.

Petroleum:

- Lobito oil terminal damaged in a South African raid 12 August, 1980.

- Luanda oil refinery damaged in a South African raid 30 November 1981, with US$21.2 million in direct damage and US$5.5 million in lost crude oil. UNITA guerillas hit the refinery again on 29 November, 1990, inflicting light damage.

- Namibe fuel storage tanks damaged in an attack by South African marines on 5 June, 1986: US$3.6 million, including damage and fuel loss.

- Huambo oil storage tanks sabotaged on 13 December 1987: US$3.2 million, including damage and fuel loss.[23]

- Other attacks on oil storage at Galinda, 1984; Quinguila (Zaire province) 1987-90 (six times); Malanje, March 1989; and a small oil well 20 km from Soyo (Zaire province) in October 1990.

in 1986 about 52,000 lines; and in 1991 about 78,000 lines. Most of this growth, it appears, was in Luanda (which will get 10,000 more lines before the end of 1992).

In sum, while the chattering classes in Luanda were more in touch with each other, subscribers up country fell ever deeper into isolation.[20]

Energy

Most modern business organizations and governments rely on a steady supply of electricity. Industry, warehousing and trans-shipment services, offices, technical and adult education, information and telecommunication systems and overall urban services cannot function effectively without power supplies. Refrigeration, security and street lighting, lifts and air conditioning, electric bread ovens and telex and fax machines are considered essential in everyday life in the cities.

Above all, most water pumps are electrically-driven. When electric current fails, as it did scores of times in Luanda and other urban areas throughout the war, the repercussions were many and severe. Public health and hygiene, already bad, worsened; women and girls spent hours trying to find water, just as in the countryside. Production lines stopped, yet workers' wages had to be paid. Tonnes of frozen fish spoiled, yet poor consumers could not afford to eat anything else. Night classes were cancelled, yet Angola needs more literate and numerate people.

The petroleum sector provides the country's main export and main source of foreign exchange. Nearly 75 percent of the central government's annual revenue derives from petroleum taxation. This sector was an economic target, during the war with almost all the sabotage incidents post-1984 and most damage, incurred in direct South African action.

Schools

No inventory of physical destruction of schools has yet been made, however, a conservative estimate would be a net loss of more than 10,000 classrooms, representing more than half those available at the beginning of the 1980s.

Accounts from just two provinces sketch the overall picture. In Lunda-Sul province: of 365 schools, 100 destroyed, mainly in rural areas.[24] Bocoio *município* Benguela province: of 22 schools, 17 destroyed.[25]

In 1981 the government reported a total national figure of 18,955 classrooms, most of them for primary education. By 1988 it could count only 10,400 — including new classrooms built during the period. The war reached new heights of destructive intensity during the period 1989 through May 1991. Extrapolation of the 1981 to 1988 net rate of loss would point to a further net loss of 2,300 formal classrooms in the period 1989 to 1991.

Deep in the bush of eastern Angola, UNITA set up classrooms as well. The most recent postwar total, according to UNITA figures, is of 835 schools.[26] The number destroyed or abandoned is unknown.

Despite continuous rebuilding and reorganizing, Angola came out of the war with only half of its formal 1981 classroom capacity intact. The cost of replacing the classrooms would be about US$67 million.[27]

Thus, despite an overall decline in school attendance since the peak in 1980, Angola's remaining classrooms are grossly overcrowded and underequipped. For many children, schooling now takes place under a tree, in an abandoned farm building, or even a shipping container.[28] The government no longer defines classrooms, but "learning spaces". In 1991, these "learning spaces", including formal classrooms, totalled 14,655. Not included in that figure were the dozens of informal, unregistered schools which have sprung up in most cities, nor the classrooms built under UNITA auspices.

Health

Diarrheal diseases, malaria, respiratory infections and measles continue to kill people at alarming rates. Infants and children

Photo 4.3: *Students in a partially re-built schoolroom at Kaimbambo, Benguela province. As yet, the school has no equipment or desks.*

are the chief victims. As shown in Chapter Two, war boosted those rates.

Increased incidence of poor health in the war years is largely explained by the collapse of public hygiene. Overcrowding in the cities (but also in settlements for displaced persons), contaminated water and food, non-functioning or non-existent latrines and enlarged mosquito-breeding areas are some of the effects of war and neglect.

They resulted from hundreds of thousands of people fleeing war zones; from water, sewage and drainage systems failing through over-use and under-maintenance; from health and urbanization policies being off-target. Such factors combined to poison the environment for everyone, rich and poor.

The war also undercut efforts to protect people from health risks and to cure them of illness.

Health Units

Angolans have never been well-served by an overall network of health services. Despite efforts by health workers on both sides, coverage became more uneven during the war years.

In 1980, only about 30 percent of the Angolan population had access to health services. The proportion at the beginning of the 1990s has not been officially estimated, but it has almost certainly declined. In Malanje province by 1988, only 33 of 101 health posts were still operating; 52 had been destroyed in guerilla attacks and the other 26 had been abandoned, since the system simply could not keep them going. In the most affected provinces by 1988, only about half of all health units were operating, the rest having been destroyed or abandoned.[29] In 1990, the Health Ministry reported the looting, destruction or closure of 92 health units, and the death or injury of 16 health workers, in 11 provinces from which reports were received.

Yet, in 1990 the government claimed to have a total of 1,606 health units, up from 1,511 in 1984. And the number of health workers had increased to 11,229 — 13 percent more than in 1984 (despite many dropping out to take up better-paying work in the informal sector). Several thousand traditional midwives had also been trained and recognized.[30]

UNITA also established a system of civilian health care. In 1989 it counted 4,781 health care workers (78 percent of them paramedics), based at 214 health units of various sizes in Kuando Kubango Province[31], plus 513 health facilities, mainly clinic posts, elsewhere.[32] Data on wartime losses of UNITA health workers and facilities are unavailable.

Vaccination Programmes

At the outset of the 1980s very few infants and pregnant women — the key at-risk people — had been immunized against the preventable killer diseases: tetanus, measles and polio. By 1989, nearly half of all one-year-olds had been innoculated against tuberculosis (up from 30 percent in 1985) but no major advances had been made over 1985 levels in the case of other innoculations (diphtheria/pertussis/tetanus; polio and measles). Innoculation rates in rural areas were especially low, in both government and UNITA-held territory.[33] Poor access due to war explains most of this continuing vulnerability to disease among Angola's rural majority.

Aids and Other Sexually-Transmitted Diseases

The mobility many Angolans lost during the war may have put a brake on the spread of Aids. But the war put people into high-risk roles — as soldiers, truck drivers and prostitutes — without their knowing the dangers and thus accelerated its spread. A study published in 1990 based on blood-testing of healthy Angolans in six provinces showed an HIV-positive rate of 9.3 per cent.[34] For purposes of comparison, the rate in Zimbabwe in 1992 approached 25 percent. With the ending of the war and deepening economic distress, efforts to educate at-risk groups and promote the use of condoms is a daunting task.

Water Supply

Only toward the end of the war were guerilla efforts aimed at cutting water supplies, the lifeline of health for urban populations. Cutting off electricity would usually stop water flows — at least for poor city dwellers with no generators to keep electric water pumps running. But cutting the supply of water itself was life-threatening. Luanda's water system was sabotaged several times, most dramatically when guerillas attacked its water treatment plant at Kifangondo in November 1990.

Damage from such attacks, plus lack of planning and maintenance, left the system in a precarious state. According to one estimate, US$9 million is needed soon to effect minimal repairs and prevent complete collapse.

In small towns the risks to public health are just as bad, if not worse, than in Luanda: "In the colonial era, many towns had small systems drawing surface water by pipe with a minimum of protection or treatment. The majority of such systems were destroyed or ceased working for lack of maintenance."[35]

Most rural people rely on streams, pools and shallow, hand-dug pits where water is close to the surface. As people and livestock were concentrated around a few such sources of water, the war then undercut public health in rural areas. In the southwestern provinces, where more than 1,000 boreholes had been drilled in the colonial era (mainly to serve cattle). Deliberate destruction, compounded by natural silting and lack of pump maintenance, denied water to more than 150,000 people and their livestock. There were reports of guerillas dropping grenades down wells, causing them to collapse.[36]

Such destruction forced people to move, which then put further pressures on already over-taxed lands and water supplies in zones of denser habitation.

Other Government Services

Many services, which governments normally provide, were curtailed or suspended due to the war.

Centres for Agricultural Research and Training

Angola has 12 such stations. One of them was the veterinary centre at Chianga, described at the beginning of this chapter. The others were also open to attack in rural areas, and most were abandoned, left to be guarded by watchmen. The flight of Portuguese technicians in 1975 left them largely devoid of persons and purpose. In the colonial era their services were mainly for settler farmers and exportable crops. The National Institute of Agronomic Research (INIA) announced in early 1992 a plan to repair and revive these centres.[37]

General Government Structures

An unknown number of state-owned buildings were destroyed or damaged during the war. The houses and offices of local government officials were special targets of attack. Following the peace accords, the government moved quickly to plan the repair of "guest houses, Government House, the Governor's official residence" in the capital of Zaire province, Mbanza-Congo[38], and, in Bie province, "seven district administration buildings, 30 other administrative posts, and 60 residences for administrators."[39]

Such re-building coincided with efforts to extend central government authority, under terms of the peace agreements, to zones out of bounds to it during the war.

Rainfall Recording Stations

In farming countries, farmers and their supportive institutions need detailed, local information on moisture levels for good management of crops and cattle. Angola inherited a network of 540 meteorological reporting stations in 1975. Due to insecurity, lack of trained staff and outright destruction, by the end of the 1980s only eight were functioning — some of the time. By March 1992, however, some 30 to 40 stations were reporting. But such information still served only a tiny fraction of Angola's farmers and support bodies.

Environment

For the Angolan environment, the war had contrary effects. As this and other chapters note, it was disastrous for the "human habitat". However, by crippling most economic activities based on advanced technologies, Angola's war helped curb damage to the environment from many of the effects of conventional "development".

Economic growth in the colonial era was, up to 1975, conventionally destructive: tropical teak forests fell to the clear-cut saw; soils in export crop zones became saturated with chemicals; and waters near cities began showing signs of industrial pollution.

With the onset of war, most of this kind of damage tapered off as plantations and factories shut down. In Lubango, for example, output from a tannery fell to a fraction of what it had been, since those who had furnished the hides could no longer sell their livestock. Previously, the tannery had poured toxic wastes into a stream used by local residents for bathing and washing clothes.

The war's most serious environmental consequence for people — especially women — stemmed from the way it rapidly redistributed population, and undercut their means to survive in new circumstances. Where people were obliged to settle in ever-larger numbers, damage to land and vegetation intensified.

The greatest ecological dramas began developing in and around Angola's urban areas. Woodfuel needs of households on the edges of towns and cities began to deplete nearby forests. This created ever-widening circles of scrubland

Parks and Wildlife - Views of a Veteran

João Seródio de Almeida, Angolan educationalist and environmentalist, is General Secretary of the Angolan Environmental Association. In the 1970s he was in charge of two of Angola's important national parks, now poised for recovery after decades of neglect. The following comments are excerpts from a wide-ranging interview by Angolan senior journalist Jose Ribeiro in February 1992.

"In my view the war was not the most important element of the current state of the environment in Angola. Much more important than the war was the period of Portuguese colonial rule. Then there was no understanding, no preparation of people to face environmental problems. The issue was not even raised in Portuguese education. The proof of this is that Portugal itself was never the subject of environmental concern.

"But why, you might ask, did the Portuguese then set up national parks in Angola? They did so because the United Nations forced them to. When the UN established the principle of nature conservation in the 1940s, and urged governments to set up parks to conserve some special ecosystems, Portugal did so to shut up the rest of the world so it could continue with its colonies.

"So they set them up, but never really supported them. The little they did was to control hunting of wild game. That was strictly a repressive activity. The wardens were there to impose fines. They never tried to educate people, to explain why it was important to protect certain species and to protect the forest.

"When independence came, the Portuguese park wardens all went back to Portugal. Why? Because most of them were agents of PIDE [the Secret Police].

"Therefore, after independence and the dismantling of Portuguese authority, Angolans thought, 'Now the land is ours. We can do what we want. There are no longer any parks, that was just an obsession of the settlers.' This was how people thought, which was different from what occurred in the lands colonized by the English, for example.

"The war has made it hard to keep up Angola's parks. I spent the year of independence at Kissama National Park, with local residents. It was very interesting. We managed to convince the local people that the park was needed nationally, and that local people themselves would benefit from a well-preserved park when the tourists started to come back. They could sell handicrafts and get jobs from tourism.

"Result: people started cooperating. They helped protect the park. Whenever poachers came in, the people came to tell me. We managed to catch a series of poachers — but only with the help of the people.

"Now, with the war, it is different. Neither I, nor my colleagues, could live alone there, in the middle of a national park. Without protection, without firearms — it was too dangerous. Moreover, there was the stigma of being repressors by not letting people hunt.

"Wildlife has suffered. Elephants, for example, accustomed to cars and people, had lost their natural defenses. They were shot easily. Other animals were targets of soldiers and guerillas, usually just for food.

"But the effect of the war was not just the direct shooting of wild animals. Rather, it was the lack of control over territory and the habitat. People — military or otherwise — came and went as they pleased. And that helped destroy the habitat of wild things. For example, early in the 1980s the army used part of the Bicuar National Park as a firing-range for big guns and explosive devices. Now the bad thing wasn't that the animals were killed or ran away. It was the destruction of the forest and other vegetation.

"Nevertheless such destruction was fortunately limited to specific points on the map. Angola is a huge land, and the points of destruction were therefore tiny relative to that massive terrain. The more serious destruction has been human and social, especially in attitudes and organization. This is what we must address."

around the cities. In most towns and some cities, women and children had to walk ever farther to the forests to fetch firewood. Much of their work was merely to collect fallen branches, not to cut down trees.

Private entrepreneurs and state companies, on the other hand, were less concerned about deforestation as they intensified their cutting of certain forests once woodfuel collection over wide areas became too risky as the war dragged on. Charcoal was the main product, supplied chiefly through parallel channels at high prices to urban consumers. Unchecked charcoal production is notoriously bad for forests.

Government policy since the early 1980s has been to encourage households to switch from wood to gas, kerosene and electricity. Such encouragement has been largely ineffective because of poor distribution systems and because cookers using those types of energy have rarely been available. Even if they were available, prices put them beyond the reach of most urban households.

Therefore pressures on Angola's forest biomass — which in aggregate terms is super-abundant, with growth exceeding by far total demand for fuelwood — are growing more intense in the vicinity of every city and town. The result is barren, eroding terrain where forests once stood.

The crisis of the urban areas (reviewed in Chapter One) is a crisis of public health and hygiene. Despite occasional efforts, city administrations have been overwhelmed by a rising number of problems, from rubbish removal, collapsing sewers and drains to mosquito and rodent control and the hygiene of kitchens serving the public. Population densities of some Angolan urban neighbourhoods exceed some parts of Calcutta and Cairo. Overcrowding in poor-quality houses is a basic environmental hazard for residents. As a result, urban administrations have been unable effectively to help the health authorities in stopping the increase of contagious disease.

In many parts of the world, bad hygiene and disease are problems mainly of poor neighbourhoods. But as recent studies conducted for UNICEF on poverty and health in Luanda have indicated, both poor *and* rich are vulnerable — so appalling is the public health environment of that city.[40]

Beyond the life-and-death consequences of such a situation, the burdens of a bad urban environment fall on women, who care for the sick.

At the root of the apparent paralysis in tackling these problems are matters of organization and training. But also at play has been government reluctance to accept citizen participation in deciding which problems should be tackled and how. Democratic urban political processes could be a major step forward in improving the urban environment.

In the countryside, the war forced people and their livestock to live in ever more limited zones, with grave environmental consequences. In many farming zones in the central highlands, for example, soils are now exhausted from too many years of use, and few means to retain or restore fertility. Crop yields are therefore dropping, year by year.

Erosion is taking an ever bigger toll on farm lands. Heavy rains in the central highlands wash away thousands of tonnes of topsoil every year. Farmers in these zones are generally skillful, and aware of the importance of fertile soils. But hunger, crowding, and lack of livestock forced many to abandon normal strategies of crop rotation and manuring.

All this puts at risk the future of farming in many areas which were once among Angola's most productive.

In pastoral zones of southwest Angola, systems of extensive grazing broke down as war encircled herding communities and hampered the recovery of cattle ranches. War and economic breakdown also curtailed the sale of oxen for plowing in farming areas, a fundamental trade link in the countryside. All this has meant increasing numbers of livestock on rangeland. Effects on traditional pastures have been devastating. It may take years for grasses to return. In the semi-arid province of Namibe, the war forced pastoralists and their herds into a corner. The resulting pressures, and natural forces such as wind, have denuded scrublands, allowing the coastal desert to encroach.

During the war, concern rose about uncontrolled, and thus excessive, fish harvests by foreign boats off Angola's shores. Whatever the basis for such concerns, threats of a different kind affected fish catches for fishing people in some of Angola's bays.

Another long-term effect on the environment in southern Angola that often goes unmentioned is the destruction of teak forests and wildlife, especially elephants.

A dossier prepared by a United States conservation group and presented to the US Congress in 1988 accused South Africa of hosting a massive international ivory smuggling operation. The Conservation, Environmental and Animal Welfare Consortium said in their report that at least half of the great elephant herds that had roamed the plains of southern Angola in numbers exceeding 200,000 had been systematically annihilated. A secret 10-month investigation by the US Attorney-General confirmed that members of the South African Defence Force (SADF) in Angola and neighbouring Namibia "have been actively engaged in killing and smuggling of wildlife species — including rhinos and elephants — for personal profit"[41]

Satellite photographs show the decimation of the great teak forests of southern Angola. And the UNITA leader, Jonas Savimbi, told a reporter from the French Magazine, *Paris Match*, in 1988, that UNITA was ordered to pay for South African assistance with ivory and teak. The cost of this is incalculable, especially in long-term effects.

In the case of the Bay of Namibe, the threat was directly related to the war. In the mid-1980s South African military frogmen sabotaged ships docked at the port of Namibe. To counter that threat, the Angolan military began a systematic effort to keep frogmen out of the bay. At regular intervals they detonated explosives underwater. Such explosions stun or even kill anyone or anything swimming below the surface. The result was the complete disappearance of fish from the Bay of Namibe, and the destruction of the livelihood of many local fishermen. The return of the fish, and the restoration of their breeding places in the bay, may take years.

Environmental threats seen in other parts of the world — chemical pollution of soils and water by big mines and plantations, massive deforestation for hardwood export, etc. — have not returned to Angola. However, they are clearly on the horizon if certain interests have their way unchecked by firm legislation and the means to enforce it.

Environmental concern and action have begun to take on new dynamism with the advent of political pluralism and new space for citizen initiative. The Angolan Environmental Association, *(Associação Angolana do Ambiente)*, a non-governmental organization for public education, took shape in the early 1990s. Together with others, it is pressing for a broad educational effort among the public, parties, and decision-makers. It advocates careful formulation of policies regarding settlement and population distribution, land rights and land use, farm practices, electrification and fuel-switching, and laws to protect natural resources. It also calls for strong state and non-governmental institutions to enforce new codes and a new ethic of care and respect for the environment in which Angolans can live healthier lives now and in the future.

5

Economic Consequences of War — and Peace

For Angolans and visitors alike, damage to public and private property is what is most obvious. From the shattered windows and overflowing sewers in the cities to the rusting carcasses of vehicles by the side of roads, the signs of physical and envioronmental decay are pervasive.

But, just beneath this ugly surface is damage of a deeper kind: the distortion of systems of exchange, the loss of people's livelihoods, living standards, and the narrowing of opportunities for the future.

In reviewing the economic consequences of the war, one must also raise a curtain on the economic consequences of the peace. This chapter addresses both these issues.

Financial Costs

Previous studies of war costs to Angola have relied on differing methods of calculation, and thus reached varying estimates. Table 5.1 (overleaf) lists some examples (in US dollars of the day).

These figures convey the scale of the burden best in light of Angola's GDP in 1980 (about US$5 billion) and its GDP in 1987 (US$7.7 billion). Its foreign debt in 1987 was estimated as US$4 billion. Of all southern African nations' war-related losses, Angola's are the greatest in absolute terms.

Despite Angola's oil wealth, its overall financial losses (including lost potential growth) have been the greatest in relation to the size of the economy — although Mozambique's losses in relation to its much poorer economy have been almost as heavy.

This section concentrates on Angolan state finances, rather than attempting an over-all summing up.

Figure 5.1 (facing page) indicates the weight of recorded defence-related spending over the years. To this would have to be added secret extra-budgetary expenditures for defence.

Data on hard currency costs of the war are not available, but the war's claims on the state's foreign exchange may be estimated. Especially in the years of the big conventional battles (1984 through 1989), goods and services acquired abroad for the war accounted for about two-thirds of what was budgetted for defence and security. In those years, cash outlays or obligations in hard currency for military ends would have equalled 40 to 50 percent of the country's yearly export earnings, and 90 to 120 percent of state tax revenues from the petroleum sector.[7]

Military outlays paid in Angolan currency for salaries, services, foodstuffs and investments (which also had foreign currency components) were also substantial. These accounted for a large part of the state's printing of money far beyond its revenues.

From time to time the state tried to dampen the inflationary effects by simply not paying the troops and others, such as teachers — a crude form of forced savings. Such moves may have slowed inflation for a while, but they also depressed morale. Late in the war years, a small but increasing number of government soldiers went "missing". That is, they

Table 5.1: Estimated Costs of War in Angola

Dates	Costs*	Observations
1975 to 1976	6.7 billion	Physical damage only
1976 to 1979	0.3 billion [1]	Physical damage only
1980 to 1985	10.5 billion [2]	Physical damage plus some economic effects
1980 to 1986	15 to 18 billion [3]	Loss of GDP (embracing all costs and losses)
1980 to 1988	30 billion [4]	Loss of GDP
1975 to 1988	22 billion [5]	Physical damage, direct economic loss and additional defense spending
1975 to 1991	20 billion [6]	Physical damage

* Costs listed are in US dollars of the day

deserted. During the 1980s over 13,000 teachers quit their jobs for other work. Angola's total teaching staff was only about 31,000 in 1990.

If a norm of four percent of GDP (sub-Saharan Africa's average for defence expenditure) is applied, "excess" spending on military purposes may be defined as the amount of expenditure above the norm.

Thus, in the period 1975-1983 Angola's excess military spending averaged US$450 million per year; in 1984-1987 the yearly excess averaged about US$800 million per year; in 1988-1991 about US$1.3 billion per year.

This means that a total of about US$ 12.5 billion was paid out of the Angolan state treasury for the military — in excess of what it would have paid out had it followed the norm of four

Figure 5.1: *Breakdown of Government Expenditures*

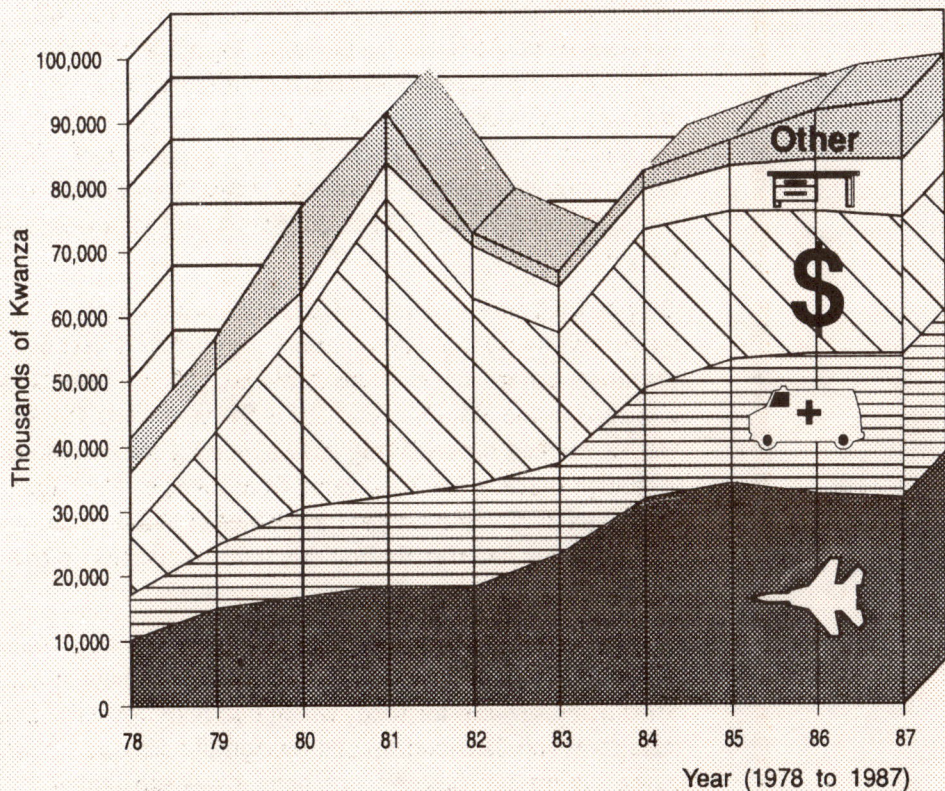

Year (1978 to 1987)

Administration $ Economic Development Social Services Defense

percent of GDP. Add to that, war-related spending budgetted in other categories, and secret expenditures, and the total would be about US$15 billion from 1975 through 1991. The immediate beneficiaries, incidentally, were chiefly *western* suppliers of matériel, lethal and otherwise.

During the 1980s, the war swallowed up directly about 60 percent of national financial resources. That left a very slim margin for savings. Such limits become even narrower in light of recent balance of payments deficits caused by purchase of commodities and services, and loan repayments.

Angola's foreign debts in 1991 stood at about US$11 billion — more than GDP in that year. Of that amount, US$4 billion was owed to the former Soviet Union, three-quarters of it thought to be military debt. The Soviet Union had earlier written off Angolan military debts incurred up to 1985.[8]

Costs incurred by the Cuban presence have not been officially revealed. Only the total cost of the Cuban withdrawal (1989-1991) was made known — US$850 million — which Angola paid for entirely. To support Cuban forces with food, matériel, and energy while in the country, Angola also paid substantial amounts. Over 377,000 troops, and 65,000 civilians from Cuba rotated through Angola from 1975 to 1991. Current estimates drawn from national and international sources indicate an average cost of US$100 million per year. Thus over 16 years, an amount of US$1.6 billion would have been involved. Added to withdrawal costs, the total bill for Cuban support would approach US$2.5 billion.

Despite high levels of self-sufficiency among people victimized by war, the government also had to divert resources toward relief of the displaced. Most of the money allocated to the State Secretariat for Social Affairs (SEAS) was earmarked for receiving and supporting the displaced. Although much of the food came from foreign relief agencies, the Angolan government paid a substantial share of the costs of purchasing and distributing this food, especially in the early years of the war.

The war-induced shift of hundreds of thousands of people to the cities placed additional demands on government spending. Most of these were for food, which had both domestic (mainly state farm and distribution) and foreign dimensions. In both cases, the foreign currency component was substantial.

More importantly, the war was partially responsible for driving up the food import bill by preventing the renewal of small-scale farming, which had produced the bulk of the country's foodstuffs in the colonial period.

Assuming conservatively that half the food import bill was due to war, Angola was forced to spend US$50 to US$100 million per year, totalling more than US$1 billion in foreign exchange. (In this sense, western grain merchants could have asked for no better means to boost sales in Angola.)

The vast expansion of Angola's urban population also increased pressures on state spending for health, education, and other social services.

Special measures for the war-injured were another obligation of state spending. Apart from local hospitalization and outpatient costs, hundreds of "special cases" were flown abroad for medical treatment and convalescence. In 1990 alone, US$2.3 million was spent on all patients abroad, most of whom were presumed to be war-injured.[9]

Assuming that five percent of government social services spending (health, education, and especially social affairs) was due to extra war-induced claims, excess government spending in this category would approach US$30 million-per-year, or about half a billion dollars over 16 years.

Costs to the Angolan government in direct spending from the treasury due to the war effort may amount to the figures shown in Table 5.2.

To put such costs in perspective, they represent about 10 times Angola's total annual foreign earnings in the late 1980s.

Table 5.2: Direct Angolan Government Spending Due to War	
Government Expenditures	Costs*
Excess defence spending	15 billion
Military loans, ex-USSR	3 billion
Cuban troop support	2,5 billion
Excess food imports	1 billion
Excess social services	0.5 billion
Total	22 billion

* Costs listed are in US dollars of the day

Spread over 16 years, this total averages slightly more than Angola's average yearly earnings from oil in those years. In other words, the war put Angola's treasury continually in a deficit position. Looked at another way, the total is about three times Angola's annual gross national product in the late 1980s.

Decades of Distortion

Out of the chaos and ashes of Angola's violent rupture with the colonial order there arose not a glorious economic phoenix but a bird of a different feather, half vulture, half dodo.

For, together with rigid forms of state socialist control, rapacious forms of private commerce and accumulation also emerged. Angolans found themselves in a two-way economy: a system of heavily subsidized and rationed goods on one side and a system of anarchic markets (with much the same goods) on the other. Stepping from one side of this looking-glass world into the other, week in, week out, is the only way many Angolans managed survival in the wartime economy.

Ample descriptions and analyses of Angola's economy can be found elsewhere.[10] A brief sketch here is, however, illustrative.

Angola's economy has always looked outward, being firmly fixed and integrated into the world system — on the *periphery*. Before it became a colony, it exported slaves and ivory. In the last 65 years of colonial rule, its lands and people were organized to export agricultural products, iron and diamonds — all produced "onshore". At the end of the colonial period, all those exports were overshadowed by petroleum produced "offshore". World prices for all these exports created a long economic boom up to the early 1970s.

This was essentially growth in enclaves and in cities. It was growth without development — and Angolans saw precious little of that growth. How and where accumulation took place were not transparent matters. Parallel markets sprang up based on coffee revenues and embezzlement by some of the Portuguese military and administrators. Malpractices, feeding both the small person's savings and the big operator's private fortunes, were rife. As the World Bank notes, remittances to Lisbon by settlers, along with over-invoicing, shifted most savings out of the colony.[11] Angola became a lucrative milk-cow, but the cream was not for most Angolans.

The economy's post-1945 boom accelerated trends which made traditional households in the countryside dependent on high-priced commodities bought in exchange for low-priced labour and rural products. For ordinary Angolans, the boom was no boon. Many became poorer and more vulnerable.[12] Eventually, pushed beyond endurance, Angolans picked up the gun to gain the right to run their own country, and to tap the stream of benefits flowing to others.

Then came 1975, and the beginning of economic collapse. Sabotage, export of goods and expertise, war damage and the absence of trained people sent the economy into a free-fall. In 1976 the new government inherited a system producing at only 60 percent of 1974 levels, and contracting fast.

The new leaders were nonetheless optimistic: the badly-skewed economy could be re-made, by dint of the state's own efforts, on all fronts.

Ideology ruled as well, and some important options were closed off. Rather than see the controlled revival of small enterprise, for example, official policy was to discourage it and, in its place, substitute a variety of cumbersome state agencies. This had crippling effects, especially for farmers. The official precept was "combat the petty bourgeoisie and expand the economic role of the state". It helped depress, and eventually push underground, many networks of exchange on which people's living standards depended. Purchasing power and, with it, incentives to produce, dropped.

By the end of the 1970s the Angolan economy was receding towards mono-production, the exhaustion of stocks and the beginning of continual scarcity *(desabastecimento)* which propelled the parallel market, long in the shadows, to centre stage. Moreover, the state itself, assailed from without and stretched far beyond its human capacities within, began to weaken — a process seen in most parts of Africa — and thus to lose its powers to serve the public good.

Candonga: The Parallel System

Having fixed prices and wages to put a subsidized floor under living standards of the formal working class and state officials, the government expected to see the economy move in an upward spiral. A key assumption was that farmers would supply urban workers, who would reciprocate with goods and services for farmers — the basis of the "worker-peasant alliance".

Instead, the cities became points of net consumption, economic islands supplied mainly from abroad. Farmers were left to fend for themselves, with few incentives to produce. By 1979 Angola was spending a quarter of its dollar earnings to import food. This included beef, even though southwest Angola's herds of beef cattle were already over-grazing their pastures.

This cumulative, self-reinforcing downward spiral stemmed from ideology and received ideas of state socialism, such as pessimistic views of small-farmer capacities and the wickedness of traders. But it also had roots in objective circumstances, such as the collapse of rural-urban transport networks, the war's destruction and terror and the strong voice of the new state class.

Regardless of which root cause one chooses — and there were many — the net result was exactly what the government said it wished to avoid: prodigious accumulation in private hands, and a commercial economy (and its potential revenues for the state treasury) out of public control.

Shortages forced goods, services and money into unregulated, untaxed channels where supply (which was short and dropping) and demand (which was high and rising) determined prices. In 1990, an urban family of five required a monthly income of 150,000 kwanzas to make ends meet, yet the salary of an average technician was only 30,000 kwanzas.

To supplement fixed wages, employees regularly re-sold goods to parallel operators. The sources of the goods were shops run by the state, those belonging to enclave companies, and foreign exchange stores; workplaces providing employees with monthly payments in kind *(auto-consumo)*; local production by farmers, fishermen and artisans; "anonymous imports" — smuggled and stolen merchandise; and especially imported goods bought legally by big operators but illicitly re-channelled from state supply systems into parallel systems. Transport services escaped most state control. In construction and repair branches, most skilled workers quit state firms to practise their trades for wages set by the "free market".

The government tried to outlaw the parallel market by setting up Economic Police to stamp it out. In early 1984 the police raided vendors at several of Luanda's marketplaces — the most visible end of the parallel system — and the workplace of the small operators. They confiscated goods, put vendors in jail, and wrecked their stands. Several people died. Later, the police also tried smashing trading networks between Luanda and up-country sources of food.

These measures backfired. There was fierce public outcry and when police mounted follow-up sorties, the market people forced them to retreat. The government then wisely, and

Figure 5.2: *Growth of Marketplaces*

Calemba

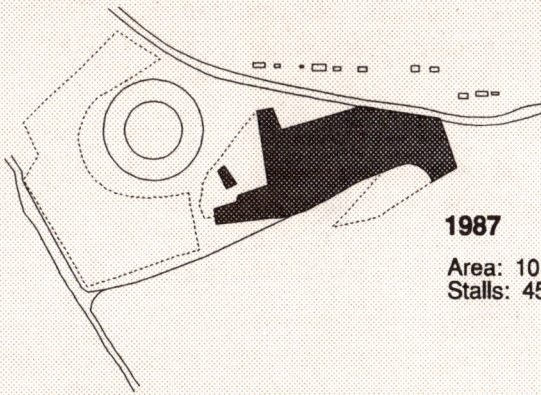

1987

Area: 10,000 m2
Stalls: 450

1989

Area with stalls: 7,000 m2
Area without stalls: 10,500 m2
Total area: 17,500 m2

Tunga N'Go

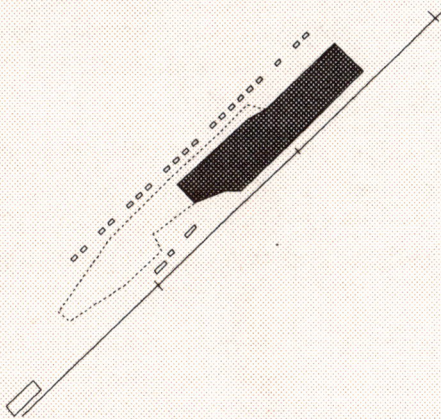

1987

Area: 12,000 m2
Stalls: 480

1989

Area with stalls: 10,000 m2
Area without stalls: 8,000 m2
Total area: 18,000 m2

Roque Santeiro

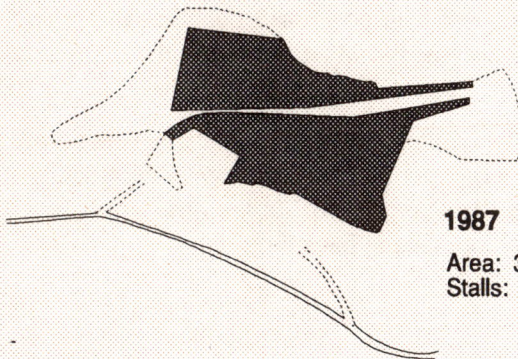

1987

Area: 32,000 m2
Stalls: 1250

1989

Area with stalls: 30,000 m2
Area without stalls: 20,000 m2
Total area: 50,000 m2

Area with stalls   Area without stalls   Houses   Railway

quietly, dropped its attempts to suppress the open markets, and tacitly agreed to tolerate, if not legalize, them.

From that point on, the parallel market grew enormously. Turnover in parallel trade (including construction and transport) in Luanda alone in 1989 was estimated to be at least twice the size of Angola's gross domestic product in that year.[13]

By 1992 government's tacit toleration of the parallel market turned into formal acceptance. In the end, the system of state command had become a mere intermediary factor. The parallel market became the real regulator of supply and demand and state agencies were effectively accomplices in parallel institutions.

Candonga, the parallel market, was a sign of popular energy and resourcefulness in response to crisis. However, from the standpoint of public welfare, it has been a very mixed blessing.

For hundreds of thousands of people *candonga* provided jobs. The problem was that this was work of low productivity, poverty-level returns and miserable conditions.

For both rich and poor consumers it provided essential goods and services. Value for money though, was poor because prices were usually far above what they should have been if supply channels were not dominated by a small number of big operators.

Candonga has helped redistribute some income, including rural areas, but its overall effect is regressive. A new class of kwanza millionaires and mafia-like operators now have strong positions within society. They are made up of those who control the major parallel businesses and agents of the state who took advantage of their positions to obtain benefits in foreign currency and goods. Most "little people" on the other hand, face very high costs, and narrow margins.

In the absence of sustained, non-speculative investment to generate jobs, a large, permanent, and desperate underclass has grown in the city shantytowns. In the rural areas, farming, herding, and fishing have become matters of dead-end survival for the minority who remain.

Reference Points: Inside or Outside Angola?

Other distortions also took root during the war years, fuelled by the aspirations of the new operators in the economy, both inside and outside the state apparatus. The class of state managers positioned itself well to control not only the flow of goods, but also capital. Here the farm-as-factory, and indeed the nation-as-factory were its models. Once again, the Angolan economy's point of reference was not inside, but beyond its borders, in the industrialized countries.

The results were policies and programmes which bore a striking resemblance to what industrial salesmen, consultants and engineers from both East and West were promoting: projects of "babylonic" size, generating few jobs for Angolans but requiring enormous amounts of machinery, raw materials, spares and expertise from abroad for a long time to come. Add to that the requirements in housing, dress, diet and leisure for the lucky few gaining jobs in these projects, and the total long-term claims on Angola's foreign earnings were substantial.

Import-export contracts, bank loans, and "turnkey" investment or service contracts became pivotal, hotly contested and commonly top-secret matters in state decision-making. The practice of receiving "commissions" for services rendered in the name of the state was commonplace. According to informed sources, these ranged up to 30 percent of a contract's value.[14] Angola's suppliers began to complain that "commissions" were too high, and thus began incorporating them into the contract price.

Related to such malpractices is over-invoicing. The scheme is simple, and difficult to control: a foreign supplier submits an invoice well in excess of the actual value of goods or services supplied; on receipt of payment, that excess is paid into the buyer's bank account abroad. Well- informed Angolan sources say that over-invoicing (which was practised widely in colonial days) reached "violent" levels during the war years.

From time to time, the government looked into charges of these rackets, and the role of senior civil servants in illicit practices. Findings have never been made public, so it is difficult to point to concrete cases. Yet no one with the least experience of the nation's economic life denies the existence of these phenomena, whose size already seems to have reached the point of being expressed as a percentage of the gross domestic product.

Angola is not in the least unique in such corrupt schemes. There is mounting evidence of malpractice, fraud and old-boys' networks tied to the former colonial power, which drain African countries of their earnings. And that is on top of the "fair" but even more costly practices of laissez-faire, which even the World Bank had to acknowledge in a recent study.[15]

"Process Five Hundred"

Five hundred Kwanzas is the fare — no matter the distance, no matter the client. No one bargains because someone took a risk and fixed the price. The price has resisted all fluctuations, staying firm through successive currency devaluations. Today, in Luanda, "Process 500" taxi fares account for thousands upon thousands of kwanzas changing hands.

It was born of the inadequacies of the city's bus service. It offers just the right links between main commercial points. Above all, it symbolizes entrepreneurial initiative on the outer fringes of public authority. It could have been called Luanda's parallel transport system, but it is only known as "Process 500".

As in other African cities, Luanda's taxis follow defined routes, picking up and letting off passengers as they go. It doesn't matter if the ride is long or short, the fare is the same. It links major marketplaces such as *"Cala Boca"* (Shut Your Mouth), *"Roque Santeiro"* (the title of a popular Brazilian TV soap opera) and *"Congoleses"*, huge

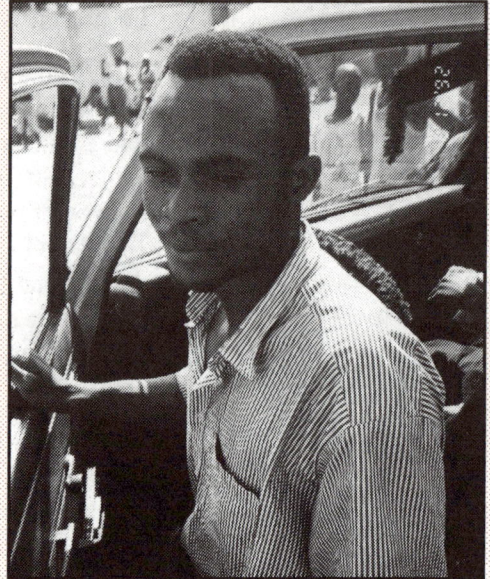

Photo 5.1: *"Process 500" taxi driver*

spaces on the edges of the shantytowns where thousands of transactions take place every day.

All taxis are in private hands and the owners usually have more than one. The driver and the conductor are responsible for their upkeep. For maintenance they go to private garages, some of which are owned by the big operators in the parallel market. There is no standard colour or model, such as in Johannesburg, where the minibus rules. In Luanda, the cabs are recognized by one or two visible features: many dents on the outside, and too many people inside.

"Process 500" taxis are one of the more lucrative parallel service industries. A 1989 study indicated that profit margins approached 60 percent of turnover — about 25 million kwanzas-a-day, equivalent to US$12,500 — for a total fleet of 500 vehicles.

The state recently tried to compete in this perfectly deregulated market, subject to perfectly limited regulations. In 1990 the government put 50 Land Rovers onto the streets of Luanda. Passengers were carried "to the door" at the reduced rate of 150 kwanzas. In a matter of months all had disappeared from the market.

Then the authorities tried other measures, including official control of the "Process 500" vehicles. Annual operating fees were established. The police were to enforce the regulations. The police and the competition, ever on the increase, are the major problems faced by this business. For the operators, there are only two attitudes for dealing with the police: either you bribe them when you don't have all your papers in order, or you pay for their approval. Says taxi driver Bocolo Daniel, 23: "It's the police that bother us. They always want money."

Bocolo has been in the business for two years. He works for an uncle from whom he earns about 85,000 kwanzas-a-week. That's 340,000-a-month — more than the official income of a senior state official with 10 years service. From his weekly salary 6,000 kwanzas are deducted for petrol, 10,000 for the conductor and 12,000 for meals. The remainder is profit. Bocolo, however, grumbles about the increasing competition, which has depressed his business.

So far, Luanda's taxi system has not fallen prey to the gangsterism and bloody mob rule which plagues similar systems in South Africa's big cities. But as things get tough, and unwanted competitors show up, the big operators may close ranks and the guns may come out.

What this meant for consumption and standards of living for ordinary Angolans, and what it might mean for the government's popular legitimacy, were evidently never given the serious consideration they deserved. Some Angolan leaders and critics outside the government called attention to the dangers (as can be read in MPLA resolutions as early as 1983) but efforts to shift things met enormous resistance, and the efforts failed.

Now the consequences of that failure have been acknowledged. As the MPLA's Governor of Huambo Province admitted in 1991, the failure helped fuel the war: "Our incapacity to satisfy the economic and social needs of the population made possible the expansion of the war of destruction."[16]

6

The Hangover of War: Mines, Crime and Violence

In the months following the Peace Accords, euphoria gave way to anxiety and fear. After a period of relative calm in which people were buoyant with the exhilaration of peace, the mood began to darken and a climate of violence and uncertainty returned. After surviving the grim years of political and military impasse, which had at least a certain predictability, the future suddenly clouded over again.

In daily life in the neighbourhood, and in national political life, Angolans were forced to confront the hangovers of war. The end of formal, overt warfare occurred in 1991 and the same year saw the beginning of new, informal violence, both public and private.

"Protracted war" was the term once used by guerilla leaders of the 20th century to sum up their strategy for liberation. The same term describes, by cruel irony, the violence that confined, terrorized, and killed people after the formal end of hostilities. Protracted war in this sense is one of anti-liberation.

Hostilities may have ended formally on 31 May 1991, but disarmament in Angola is still a distant prospect. Bullets still rest in their chambers waiting to be fired; mines still lurk in the ground ready to explode. In many minds there is a question: do those who loaded those bullets and buried those mines still intend to see them triggered?

Mines and Mine-Clearing

Angolans share with Afghanis and Cambodians and their brothers and sisters in Mozambique, the terrifying reality of living on lands infested with explosive mines.

Estimates of the total number of mines planted in Angola vary enormously, from 60,000 to "at least a million".[1] Four different armies — those of the Government, UNITA, the Cubans and the South Africans — laid mines at different times from 1975 to mid-1991. Before them, the Portuguese army, which began its offensive in 1961, buried *their* lethal devices.

Knowledge of the number of mines, and their locations, is poor. In principle, military records showing total numbers supplied, reduced by the numbers held in stock, should yield a summary figure. But military commanders admit they have no real idea about total numbers, especially in fiercely-contested zones. Official estimates for Kuando Kubango province, for example, vary from "over 15,000" in the entire province to 330,000 in just one district.[2]

More important to know, but less likely to have been recorded, were the locations. This is of special importance in Angola, where many of the mines are plastic, making them much more difficult to find by conventional detectors. Accurate mapping of mine fields was seldom done and what charts there are, difficult to find. Around Cuito Cuanavale, officials were confident of locating only a quarter of the 330,000 thought to have been laid.

Nevertheless, the sharing between former belligerents of what maps do exist was one of the first steps toward concrete peacemaking in 1991. South African and Cuban army commanders offered to furnish their maps.

But in war, maps and memories are easily shredded. Some false diagrams were drawn up to deceive opponents. Mines laid have ways of posing a new menace over time. In early 1992, United Nations monitors reported that "heavy rains have had a collateral effect of causing an increase in anti-personnel mine accidents due to soil erosion by water."[3] Roadways thought to have been cleared of mines once again become dangerous.

The picture emerging from the stream of anecdotes and contradictory announcements was of a landscape littered with large and small mines. In some areas, such as the battlefields of the southeast and the contested terrain along the railway line in eastern Bie Province, the ground is saturated with them.

Mine-clearing activities began at once following the ceasefire. Between June and September 1991, a total of 22,124 mines were deactivated, according to the National Demining Commission.[4] Government and UNITA forces teamed up in many provinces to do this dangerous work, mainly along key roads. Maps were recent, memories of mine locations were fresh, and the work proceeded apace. Sappers even came across mines laid by the Portuguese before 1975.

Once the main traffic arteries were, more or less, cleared, demining then slowed down. In some places work was suspended altogether, mainly for lack of equipment and trained personnel. In January 1992 Luanda radio announced the suspension of demining in Kuando Kubango province "due to the complex nature of the mine fields" requiring new disarming techniques and the re- training of UNITA and government sappers. Up to mid-1992, at least eight soldiers were killed and 25 were injured in mine-lifting operations.

Mine-clearing specialists emphasize the importance of avoiding all amateurism in de-mining programmes. A good de-mining programme, they insist, will *destroy* mines, not just deactivate them; otherwise they could easily enter the lucrative black market trade in second-hand arms. A basic aim must be to rebuild people's sense of security when travelling and, in rural zones, their confidence in the land. To claim to have cleared ground only later to be shown to have failed to clear *all* mines is to invite a lack of confidence among local people. This is logical and rational. If local

---

Explosive Mines: Post-War Demining Progress

Cuito Cuanvale: Of 330,000 mines thought to have been laid in the district of Cuito Cuanavale, the location of only 80,000 is known. The other quarter-million mines' whereabouts remain to be discovered. (Jornal de Angola, 28 July, 1991)

Malanje Province: Sappers from joint Government/UNITA brigades deactivated 320 mines in the province in the period June-July 1991. (Jornal de Angola, 1 August, 1991)

Zaire Province: Minesweeping operations ended along major roads in the province in early August 1991. In the period June-July, 25 anti-personnel mines and two anti-tank mines were deactivated. (Jornal de Angola, 14 August, 1991)

Kwanza Norte Province: 415 mines, of which 400 were anti-personnel mines, were deactivated in the province in the period June to July 1991, chiefly along major roads. (Jornal de Angola, 16 August, 1991)

Uige Province: 807 mines were deactivated during the minesweeping campaign in Uige, 7 July to mid-August 1991, by government troops in areas they had controlled during the war. A contingent of UNITA soldiers was expected to begin work, so that mines laid by them could be deactivated. (Jornal de Angola, 20 August, 1991)

"Eastern Front": In the provinces of Lunda-Norte, Lunda-Sul and Moxico, 4,000 mines were deactivated, as well as 377 "heavy armed projectiles", 278 hand grenades and 27 bombs, according to the government army commander of that zone. (Jornal de Angola, 26 March, 1992)

people experience the (often fatal) results of incompetent de-mining, they will stay off their land forever, even if subsequent de-mining sweeps the terrain well and truly clean. Hence the stress laid on suitably trained and equipped people.[5]

By early 1992 a team of British instructors was at work in Angola training UNITA and MPLA soldiers in de-mining methods using sophisticated sensing equipment.[6] Cuban and South African military specialists were also expected to assist in upgrading capacities of Angola's new joint armed forces.

Mines: The Costs Continue to Mount

From 1975 through mid-1991, the government recorded 6,728 incidents involving mines presumably laid by its opponents. This figure probably refers only to incidents involving soldiers.

In any event, that figure clearly understates the number of mines detonated. By 1988 the government had more than 13,000 persons recorded as missing one or both legs. Total amputees at the time was thought to be three to four times that number. Current estimates, combining official data with that of church hospitals and humanitarian agencies, are of 70,000 amputees.[7]

Meanwhile, the explosions go on, killing and mutilating scores of people every month. Typical was a news item in March 1992 from Sumbe, Kwanza Sul province:

"Joaquim Miranda Correia, a cyclist passing the National Petroleum Institute (a heavily mined location due to its strategic importance) set off a mine and lost his left leg; José Azevedo, while helping a family member find luggage after a vehicle accident, triggered a mine next to the bridge where the accident occurred. He lost his right leg."[8]

Apart from the physical and emotional costs to tens of thousands of Angolans and their families, are the costs of delay, if not total loss, to Angola's economic and social recovery.

In the countryside mines continue to serve their main function of intimidation. Through terror, they deny farmers and herdsmen mobility and access to fields and pastures. The fear and hopelessness created by the mines helped push hundreds of thousands to seek sanctuary in towns and cities. They continue to discourage most from ever returning.

Smaller access roads linking farms with commercial centres are mined and still impassable. Farmers may produce surpluses for sale, but the foodstuffs rot for want of a truck or a bus to take them to market.

Mines planted along high-tension electricity lines to deter guerilla activities now prevent repair crews from replacing the hundreds of pylons brought down, despite the mines, by sabotage. Where repair crews fear to tread, other things creep up, literally, to hinder their work: along the Lucala River, tropical vines have engulfed power lines and pylons serving Luanda.[9]

In the Bicuar Wildlife Reserve in southern Angola, wandering elephants set off powerful anti- tank mines.[10] Such dangers put in question the restoration of Angola's ravaged national parks in the short term and their attraction for tourists in the longer term.

Against mines there is little that ordinary people can do. Their livestock could be used deliberately to set off mines, but farmers are unlikely to sacrifice their herds in an amateur attempt to clear their fields. A substantial, professional programme is needed. In the meantime, many parts of Angola must remain zones in which few people can move freely.

Post-Accord Political Violence

The Peace Accords held that peace and freedom of political activity should come to all corners of Angola. In the year that followed, both sides repeatedly broke both the letter and spirit of the agreements. There were bare-knuckled fights and

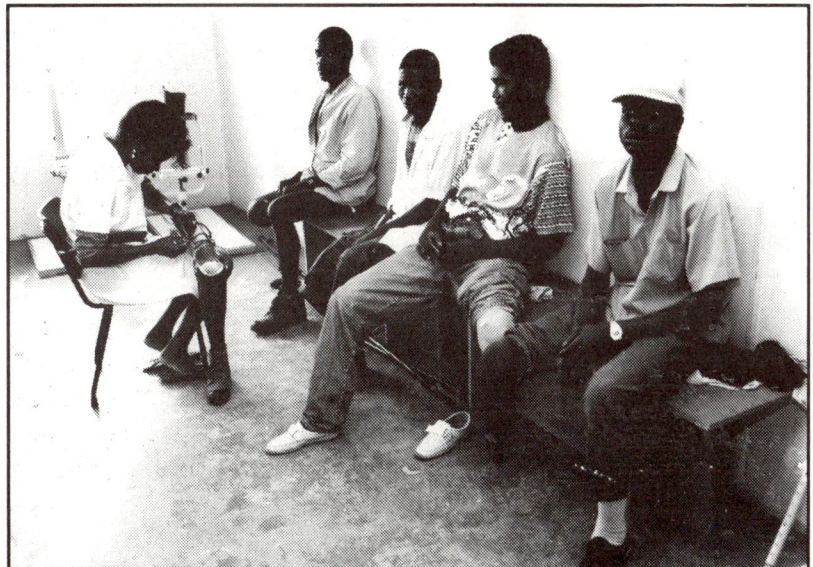

Photo 6.1: *Amputees having their artificial legs adjusted at a Red Cross health centre in a suburb of Luanda.*

armed skirmishes. To foreign and local observers these breaches were never serious enough to suspend all peacemaking processes, but for ordinary Angolans the political violence may often have seemed like the continuation of war by other means.

Implicit in the settlement was the re-establishment of state administration across the country. By the end of the war, central government authority had disappeared in as many as 50 of Angola's 163 *municípios* (districts). UNITA's military command held sway in most of these. The rest were simply unserviced, lawless territories.

In the closing months of the war, both sides pushed hard to gain or retain territory. Although it failed in its attempt to capture Luena, the capital of Moxico Province, UNITA took over many lower-level administrative towns in this period.

After the cease-fire, in difficult, province-by-province negotiations, commanders and political officials reached agreements to resume local government tasks backed by central state authority. This process crept forward with many delays and reversals. In some small towns, it worked well. MPLA and UNITA officials took part in peace ceremonies, offering speeches with conciliatory rhetoric: "We are all brothers", said a state official at a gathering at Cambundi Catembo in Malanje province,

"And we are all engaged in one common task — the pacification of minds and the consolidation of peace."[11]

Often, though, such tranquility was short-lived. In some *municípios*, UNITA re-took local government offices and sent their MPLA incumbents packing. In many others, UNITA refused to relinquish power on a variety of pretexts. In one *município*, a UNITA representative said that the central government was not welcome because "it is going corrupt the population."[12]

In early March 1992, a government spokesman said that a central state presence had been re-established in only 23 percent of the areas held by UNITA at the time of the peace agreement.

At stake was the registration of voters and the holding of elections. On this point the government was clear: where local government could not operate, there would be no registration and, therefore, no voting. Area by area, the two sides reached compromises. When the impasse would end was uncertain.

While the painfully slow talks proceeded among local commanders and politicians behind closed doors, tensions out in the streets often boiled over.

Name-calling and rude gestures quickly led to open mêlées which in turn led to armed skirmishes and reprisal murders. To wear a political T-shirt or put up a political sign was to invite a fist-fight or worse.

There were scores of ugly incidents: on 21 January 1992, unarmed UNITA soldiers and MPLA supporters in Kibala, Kwanza Sul province, first traded insults and then began brawling. Seventeen were injured, and the local MPLA offices ransacked. In mid-February 1992, 57 people were injured in disturbances in Uige province as UNITA and MPLA supporters battled each other in the streets.

The government and UNITA later reached an agreement to work together to confiscate firearms in the hands of local citizens.[13]

Police forces, usually under strength in personnel, training and equipment, were openly scoffed at and accused of pro-government bias. Since they had become the only force legally permitted to carry firearms, however, their neutrality and general behaviour became matters of intense public concern. Commissions composed of MPLA and UNITA officials were set up to monitor and discipline the police to ensure their political neutrality and objectivity. In some areas, though, confidence in the police was almost non-existent and suspected members of the secret police (DISA) were special targets for public anger and anti-MPLA agitation.

In January 1992, the Joint Political-Military Commission created to supervise the peace moved to stem the violence. It set up a Monitoring Task Group to cool tempers, discipline troublemakers and come to grips with a spiralling internal trade in arms and ammunition. No easy tasks.

Angolans did not invent political intimidation, as anyone from Beijing to Boston to Belfast can attest, but tempers heated by 16 years of fratricidal war and easy access to firearms kept tensions high.

Angolans have had little experience in problem-solving of this kind, other than the authoritarian models available to them from the colonial and post-colonial eras.

Tragically, some local options within Angola's own cultures were closed off. Long-standing methods of settling conflicting claims among neighbours and family members could have been used to cope with post-war disputes. Because the authority figures who know and practice these customary codes were manipulated or swept to one side by colonial administrators, and later by political bosses from both camps, the mechanism was damaged beyond repair. The war impoverished not only the local Angolan economy, but also its local means of conflict resolution.

Crime: The Freelance Wars

The weapons on Angola's battlefields have been silent, but on its rural highways and city streets, people may have noticed little difference. Violence and pillage spilled over into civilian life with increasing savagery in the post-war period.

Armed robberies, assaults, rapes and murders, as well as burglary and theft increased steadily. In Luanda's hospitals, deaths from violence began equalling deaths from disease. Said Afonso Ngonda of the Angolan YMCA (*Associacao Crista da Mocidade*): "The population lived practically under war, got hold of guns and has that mentality well rooted. To kill someone now is as common as killing any animal. People lost sensitivity and react with a gun, for anything or nothing."[14]

Luanda's police detailed 20,370 crimes in 1991, including more than 1,000 murders. The city's crime rate of about 81 per 1,000 residents is well above that of Europe's crime capital, London, with about 65 per 1,000 in 1990 but well below such cities as Johannesburg and New York.

Most of Luanda's crime was reported from its shantytowns. Once again, poor people are the chief victims.

In the countryside, a new breed of highwayman began robbing travellers, usually at gunpoint. On most inter-city roads, motorists were advised to travel with other vehicles, and never travel at night. Routes leading south and east from Luanda became hazardous by late 1991. Trucks and passenger autos faced risks of robbery and murder on heavily-trafficked routes such as Sumbe-Lobito, Lobito-Canjala (10 recorded attacks, January to mid-February 1992), and Malanje-Saurimo (eight attacks from May 1991 to February 1992). Not coincidentally, these were sites of some of the most bitter fighting during the war years.

Victims often reported that their attackers wore military uniforms, and carried army-issue firearms. Most attacks took place in areas close to assembly camps of soldiers waiting for demobilization.

Many indications suggest that the robber gangs were deserters, temporary or otherwise, from their assigned assembly camps.

Even in rural backwaters, such as the northern districts of Uige Province, armed gangs terrorized travellers and villagers alike in the post-war period. Rape and kidnapping occurred with alarming frequency. Areas bordering the Republic of Zaire, such as Kuilo-Kuango and Alto-Sanza, were described as "permanently in the hands of armed men."[15] The time of the freelance guerilla had arrived.

In zones of high risk to travellers such as Canjala in Benguela province, a variety of weapons and explosives were on offer from local underground arms dealers. Sidearms, TNT and even mines could be bought if one had a "good contact".[16] Arms in circulation no doubt number in the tens of thousands, if not more. Many were thought to have been hidden by soldiers before reporting to assembly camps. From time to time, arms caches were discovered and confiscated, usually thanks to tip-offs from local residents.[17]

As with most merchandise in Angola, weapons gravitated to the cities, where police efforts to confiscate them largely failed. A big problem, as Luanda's police commander has admitted, was the corruption of the police or their direct involvement in crime. For their part, police complained that the post-war rules permitting free movement of persons and goods tied their hands, since they were allowed to check only the papers of vehicles and their drivers, not the cargo. After an initial "passive" approach to confiscation of arms, 1992 was to see an "active" phase, in which police agents were expected to show "other behaviour" than before.[18]

Mediocre police protection, frustration with the criminal justice system and just plain rage led some city people to deal directly with unarmed petty criminals. Spontaneous public burnings — *carbonização* — of suspected thieves became commonplace events in shantytowns and public markets. Luanda police reported 27 cases of persons being burned alive in the five weeks beginning 1 November 1991. Ten instigators of this vigilante mob justice were arrested in the same period.[19]

As Angola concluded its first year of "peace", fear and cynicism threatened to infect people, like one of Luanda's many contagious diseases. An Angolan journalist summed up the causes and consequences: "People cease to be respected as human beings, giving rise above all to violence. Thousands of young men educated and armed to serve in combat end up in the cities. They take with them their bloody livelihoods."[20]

A war of sorts has continued in Angola long past the signing of the Peace Accords. This had political consequences too. With so much anxiety and uncertainty among Angolans, analysts sensed that many voters would vote more out of fear than hope, and many could be swayed by candidates whose solution was simply "law-and-order".

7

New Liberties,
New Forces

By April 1990, serious talks had begun in Portugal, between UNITA and Government representatives -- mediated by Portugal, the United States and other western powers, and the Soviet Union -- leading to formal signing of the Peace Accords a year later, in May 1991.

However, the shifts in Angolan political life extend beyond peacemaking between the two belligerents. They have to do with a relaxation of anxieties and antagonisms -- born of war and external threats -- and an acceptance of dissent, publicly expressed. The changes are illustrated, in part, by the official response toward small but zealous religious and political groupings.

How could such an about-face take place in such a short time? The process had begun haltingly in the late 1970s. First intellectuals, writers and artists, then church leaders and disenfranchised politicians began voicing the need for more room to speak out.

The effort had its risks. Angolans *were* dying daily in a terrible war. Angola *was*, indeed, a target for subversion, dirty tricks and disinformation, as ex-agents of the US and South African intelligence agencies, and committees of the United States Congress, had revealed. Any prudent and responsible government could not ignore such threats.

It was not easy for Angola's early proponents of civil and political rights within a pluralistic society to shrug off accusations of disloyalty and sedition, especially when the penalties for conviction could be severe. There were profound risks, but a few were prepared to take them.

Some early moves toward a more open society occurred in 1984. The government revived its 1978 amnesty campaign, this time mainly to achieve reconciliation with the FNLA. As a result, in the period 1985-1988 some 60,000 to 80,000 Angolans, including FNLA officers, emerged from forest hideouts in northern Angola and from exile in Zaire. In order to entice some of them back, jobs were created in the civil service and state enterprises. Others were absorbed in commerce or returned to their home areas. A series of gestures toward traditional authorities in rural areas also began. The government tried to involve the *sobas* more actively in local administration and settling disputes.

As the thaw set in, more and more Angolan citizens were emboldened to organize to speak out against the war and create more room for collective action.

Popular frustration with the lack of progress towards peace began to approach a breaking point in mid-1989 after the failure of the Gabadolite "peace agreement". The pact was mediated by President Mobutu Sese Seko of Zaire as a means of polishing his tarnished image as a greedy despot who systematically siphoned off Western donor monies into his own overseas bank accounts. Church leaders, intellectuals and journalists held meetings and decided to pressure both sides to end the war. There was a sense by now in which war and peace were too important to be left to the political deal-makers. Other actors had to enter the scene, whatever the risks.

Photo 7.1: *The banner of the PRD (Democratic Renewal Party) in Luanda. It reads "Power empties out citizens' rights to a free choice".*

Representatives of the Protestant churches urged the government and UNITA to begin a serious search for reconciliation. The powerful Roman Catholic bishops issued a letter to be read in all churches in November of 1989, calling on UNITA and the MPLA to stop the war and hold free elections.

Such a plea could not be easily ignored. The Catholic Church in Angola is massive and well-organized.[1] Two months later, the Angolan Civic Association (ACA) was formally launched under leadership closely linked with the Catholic Church. At the top of its agenda were practical good works and pressure on both sides of the conflict to respect human rights.

Although it had the informal approval of some MPLA leaders, the government at first moved to outlaw this new manifestation of change -- an independent group combining welfare with lobby work. The ACA prevailed and, within a year, those who had blocked ACA's registration were overruled and the Association was legalized.

Free at Last

In the stony desert along Angola's southern Atlantic coast stands the former Portuguese internment camp, Saint Nicholas. Renamed Bentiaba after independence, it became one of the country's centres of "re-education and production" -- a medium-security prison. From this desolate place, 17 Angolans held for political offences walked free on 17 July 1991.[2]

Thirteen of those freed were members of the Church of Our Lord Jesus Christ on Earth, or *Tocoístas,* a sect based on Protestant and traditional African beliefs.

In 1986, a number had been sentenced to long prison terms for plotting against state security. In 1987 at least 35 *Tocoístas* were shot dead and scores wounded when they demonstrated outside the Luanda prison where fellow church members were then held.

The other four released on that July day in 1991 were members of the Movement for Socialist Unity in Angola (MUSA), a group related to the largely Kikongo-speaking *Tocoístas.* A court had sent them to prison in early 1987, likewise for offences against the state. Arrests of MUSA members coincided with a campaign by the "Democratic Independents", yet another group whose platform included an end to the war, freeing of political prisoners and the holding of elections within two years.[3]

All 17 were freed under terms of an amnesty law introduced on 15 July 1991, during a time when liberalization measures followed rapidly one after another, and both sides in the conflict had begun to release political prisoners in terms of the Peace Accord.

On returning to Luanda, the ex-prisoners must have been astonished at what they saw. Stretched across major avenues were banners advocating the very things for which they had been sent to prison. The press, too, carried articles -- more muted perhaps -- but with similar messages: vigorous endorsement of the exercise of political freedoms; critiques of social inequalities; condemnation of imprisonment for political offences; and a welcome, even if clouded by doubts about its feasibility, of the right to vote in open elections.

The 1990s: "Political Decompression"

Debates within the MPLA intensified and came to the surface. The party named 1990 as the "Year of Enlargement of Democracy". Politically, the party could no longer maintain control over the organs of civil society by granting monopolies to its own sub-divisions in signing-up and speaking for women, youth, wage-earners, small farmers and the like. The terms used by foreign and local analysts were "opening" and "political decompression".

By December of that year, the MPLA announced not just its toleration of citizen action free of party and state supervision, but its intention "to stimulate the creation of new socio-professional associations, cultural, civic and other non-governmental organizations which compete for citizens' democratic participation."[4]

In a sense the leadership was offering a new definition of what it means to be a good Angolan. No longer was a good Angolan only a dedicated worker, a member of *o povo trabalhador* -- "The People Industrious". Nor was a good Angolan only a patriot, a defender of the cause of national unity, and member of *um só povo* -- "The People United".

Important as both those symbolic roles were, the leadership seemed to hark back to an earlier era when, in the cause of anti-colonial struggle, the good Angolan was someone who was mobilized for political battle, a member of *o povo organizado* -- "The People Organized".

Now there was a new dimension. Angolans were invited to organize themselves in their *own ways* -- out of self-interest, conviction, or neighbourly spirit. The good Angolan was now not only a good worker, nationalist and political militant, but also an active member of civil society. Implicitly, he or she was also tolerant of the next person's opinions, activities and affiliations.

The cynical may have seen this move as a sign of political cunning, an effort to tilt the playing field against those in UNITA, who would wish to constrain and colonize civil society in *their* way.

Whatever the rationale, the MPLA's call in December 1990 to go forth and populate Angola's political and civic space was met by a burst of organization-building. As many as 60 political parties emerged in the months following the moves toward multi-partyism.[5]

Sudden strikes or work stoppages raised the prospect of the appearance of new trade unions. Some members of government did not like this unaccustomed spontaneity, but took working class action in stride and came quickly to understandings.

New non-governmental organizations began blooming like wildflowers: residents' and neighbourhood groups, environmental committees, trade and professional associations, women's organizations, sports clubs, regional development associations and development service organizations, numerous charities and welfare agencies -- the list grew by the month.

Many were ephemeral things, destined to disappear within a year, but others survived, and a few began growing in membership and public profile.

New liberties in Angola go beyond the freedom to organize. In 1991 and 1992 new laws were introduced and norms encouraged to define the legal and political widening of civil society. New rules for the state and people's access to its power needed definition.

Freedom of Movement

The Angolan Peace Accords stipulate an end to "unjustified restrictions on the free circulation of persons and goods".

For its part, the government dropped its requirement that travellers between major points must produce on demand a *guia de marcha* or travel permit. This hated practice, inherited from the Portuguese, gave petty officials means to harass and detain normal citizens -- and thus extort money from them. Only in the diamond-rich area of Lunda Norte Province (Angola's Klondike, a natural magnet for smugglers) is the *guia de marcha* still required.

Throughout 1991, as peace took hold, the government phased out police and army checkpoints along major roads in most parts of the country. In March 1992 the authorities lifted Luanda's midnight to dawn curfew, in force since the attempted coup of 1977. In April 1992 visas for Angolan citizens wishing to leave or enter the country were abolished.

According to informed observers, the same did not apply in UNITA-held territory in the months following the Peace Accords. Movement of persons and goods was generally restricted and relaxation of controls followed slowly.

Movement of goods was also controlled in government territory. In Bie Province in 1991, for example, ordinary citizens were permitted to carry freely only 10 kilos of rice and meal, five kilos of rice and beans, six blocks of soap, five litres of cooking oil, two tins of powdered milk and two jugs of wine.[6] Possession in excess of those amounts presumably made any traveller a merchant, and thus subject to different regulations.

Papers and rules aside, Angolans have for years continued to travel inside and outside the country, even during the worst of the war, and generally, on their own terms. Bluff, cunning and courage have taken them a long way. The greatest impediments to their mobility were the sheer physical facts of danger and broken-down means of transport to move across an enormous and difficult landscape.

Freedom of Association

The Peace Accords single out the right to associate freely as a fundamental principle for the promotion of peace. The government gave up its claims to a hegemonic position in civil society when it approved, in March 1991, a Law on Associations. A few days later it ratified a Law on Political Parties, confirming MPLA resolutions favouring a multi-party system "based on national unity and pluralism of ideas."

These new laws marked historical turning-points for those interested in forming parties or groups in the secular world.

In the ecclesiastical world, their importance is less -- for churches and sects have been multiplying and dividing at an increasing rate since the middle of the century, undaunted by official anxieties.

Church members were certainly among victims of armed conflict, especially those moving by road in the country-side.[7] The *Tocoistas* and a few others may have met harassment, but most Angolan churches emerged from the war years with substantial membership increases.

Reconciliation with the state proceeded smoothly. Ownership of property seized from the churches was restored. Buildings used as warehouses or centres for political education again became centres of worship. The Catholic church is moving ahead with plans to establish its own university, and resume radio broadcasting.

Media Freedom

As in all wars, the Angolan belligerents had the same approach to public media -- to bend the facts to suit their purposes. The MPLA had an upper hand with its national radio and television networks, and its national newspaper. Both parties held tight control over information, not as a responsibility of government, much less civil society, but rather a matter for the *party*. Print and electronic media had to reflect party points of view.

Former adherents of both groups turned against their parties precisely because of manipulation of information. "Compulsive liars" says one of UNITA. "Censors" says another of the MPLA.[8] Information and who manages it, as in most countries, is an issue of extreme sensitivity in Angola today.

Angolan writers now face many opportunities, but wonder what to do with these new freedoms if there is little paper, ink and other supplies. Ambitions to launch new periodicals or newspapers collide at once with lack of management know-how. Radio may, for these reasons, emerge as the most dynamic news media in the coming years. Moreover, radio reaches many more Angolans than the printed word. At independence there were about 20 receivers per 1,000 persons; in 1987 there were about 50. The government has moved to depoliticize radio, but the UNITA radio — "Voice of Resistance of the Black Cockerel" — continues to broadcast.

A Bill of Rights

At the Multiparty Conference held in Luanda in January 1992 the Government launched a trial balloon: a bill of rights within a revised constitution. Attracting attention were proposals to:

- abolish the death penalty;

- outlaw torture and cruel, inhuman or degrading punishments;

- establish the right to be informed, at the time of arrest, of the reasons for one's arrest;

- limit the duration of preventive detention;

- establish the right of compensation for illegal imprisonment;

- establish the right of prisoners or detainees to receive visitors and to communicate with the world outside.

If adopted, such rights would make Angola's formal climate of civil liberties among the most liberal in the world. But how would they be enforced? Their adoption would require, according to seasoned observers, a total change of Angola's criminal justice system. The courts, public prosecutor's office and Criminal Investigation Police would need a complete overhaul. A legal end to conscription in the army or militia would mean a complete halt to past practices (by both sides), such as recruitment by press-ganging and indefinite periods of active duty. To start such a radical remodelling, like so many other changes in Angola, takes time. Nearly a year after the government passed legislation to guarantee the independence of courts and judges, one commentator wrote, "It's a secret to no one, for example, that Angolan courts are only now able to make fully concrete the principle of their independence."[9]

There is yet to appear a "culture of rights" to counterbalance the persistent, and at times heavy-handed emphasis on *duties* -- duties to the State, to the boss, to the husband, to the church. Will countervailing power -- a power counter-posed to the prevailing orthodoxies and entrenched positions of power -- emerge from Angola's still embryonic civil society?

Response to the Openings in Civil Society

Many more Angolans are now physically urbanized than before the war, but most Angolans remain bound by norms and relationships which are essentially agrarian. Most Angolans, for example, think first of order and security and would favour the restrictive codes of behaviour which have guaranteed such things in the past. For people on the edge of survival, where respect for ancestral forces is a fundamental virtue, such issues as liberties for individuals and groups to organize are rarely topmost on the agenda.

In Latin America and Asia, self-organization among poor farmers and shantytown dwellers is a right to be defended and to be extended to others. Equivalent segments of Angolan society appear to be some years away from that point -- though it may arrive sooner than anyone may now imagine.

The emergence of civil society as a point of leverage and influence in public life continues to be difficult.[11] But it seems more difficult for some people than for others.

Which actors in civil society seem more likely to endure and exercise influence on public policy? Which will be pushed to the margins or domesticated? Some seem likely at least to remain vocal and in the public eye, while others remain invisible or inaudible.

The matter is important if Angola's political leadership and processes are to evolve in ways that build strong institutions that will block totalitarian temptations and violent confrontation. In this way a democratic culture may have a chance to take root and political elites cannot settle into dynastic regimes. Instead, they could be turned out of office as a matter of right by the voters.

Some projections are possible, grouped in four categories : the strong but silent; the weak and silent; the weak but audible; and the strong and audible.

Strong and Silent: Family and Clan Ties

Ties of blood and ethnicity remain the bedrock of Angolan society. For those uprooted by war and economic necessity, the safest place to be was among kinfolk. Access to goods, housing and jobs often depends on skillful use of such ties. Those without them lost out.

The war put these family ties under severe strain and many of them broke under the pressure. Facing unprecedented stress, many Angolan families have become fragile.[12] In urban settings, parental authority and conventional norms regarding

---

Legal Help for Battered Women

For police and courts to defend the individual is not a straightforward matter in Angola. For poor women, who are at the receiving end of violence and abuse, this is especially true. That men beat their wives and girlfriends -- and children-- is common knowledge, as it is the world over. The tragedy is that, as family ties and norms break down under the wartime stress and economic decline, violence against women occurs more and more often.

One modest response is a Legal Centre in a poor Luanda neighbourhood called "Patrice Lumumba". Founded in 1984 by several lawyers associated with the Organization of Angolan Women, it sees 20 or more cases a month. Three women trained in the basics of law, the role of police and courts and administrative procedures, work at the Centre. Four women lawyers, each working one afternoon a week, provide legal counsel. A consulting doctor is sometimes called in.

The most common complaint is physical aggression. Battering of women occurs in all social classes. One aspect of the problem centres on male ego and the economics of family survival. In cities, women must earn money. Independent female control of income threatens macho self-esteem. Frustration and aggression follow. Alcohol abuse and philandering no doubt also play their parts. The acute housing shortage and a desperate everyone-for-themselves survival in the cities means that few women have the option to quit the abusive partner.

The Patrice Lumumba Legal Centre cannot solve the housing problem. Its usual method is first to see if reconciliation is possible before bringing the weight of police and courts to bear. If a case goes to court, legal assistance is provided. In cases of divorce, getting ex-husbands to help support children is a major headache, even where a court rules that they must pay.

Such initiatives as the Legal Centre provide relief to victims. But where will the ounce of prevention come from, and how will the victimization be curbed? More likely than not, by women and men translating this exposure to ugly realities into platforms of advocacy and action. From that may come necessary legislation and the means to enforce it. In this work, Angolans are showing no signs of giving up.

sexuality and marriage have eroded rapidly. Rates of teenage pregnancy have risen.

In the countryside there are also reports of social breakdowns -- including outright abandonment of wives, children and old people -- suggesting tragic levels of stress and upheaval.

The war's impact on such intimate family levels of society are still poorly known, although everyone has anecdotal knowledge. Through rapid urbanization, militarization and "forced recruitment" into petty trade, many more Angolans have struck up new ties which cut across clans and ethnic affiliation. Marriages between people from different ethnic groups are increasingly common.

As people are forced to succumb to the individualizing pressures of markets for their labour, and the daily struggle for the basics of life, reciprocal obligations to other family members are weakened. The war forced people to look for solidarity as never before, but it pushed family ties past the breaking-point.

The extended Angolan family is still intact, but crumbling at the edges. The war may not have started such trends, but it certainly accelerated and distorted them. A recovery benefiting the majority in Angola will take its best features into account -- social solidarity, preservation of local knowledge for survival and local culture for self-esteem. The foundations of a positive civil society will also depend on those key features of traditional family life.

What powers will families exercise on those who govern? Decision-making at the top has often been pushed or restrained by ties of kin at the bottom. A voice of protest or appeal from far away, through the right family channel, has been known to free someone from jail or clinch a government contract. Those myriad ties, tugging on the hearts or political calculations of people in leading positions, will persist. Not yet known is how much impact they will continue to have on public policy-making.

Equally plausible is that, as Angolan politics shift, links of money and power will displace the blood-ties of family. The shrewd business alliance, or political machine, may become the model. In the place of family bonds could come chains of patrons -- bosses, politicians, kingpins in the parallel market -- and clients in need of protection. Hence the talk of "gangsterization" in Angolan private and public life.[12]

Weak and Silent: Informal Workers

Those pushed to the margins of the economy are unlikely to gain roles in, or benefits from, the new civil society. Only in exceptional times and places will they gain "voice" to influence decision-making. Among those categories are:

Small Farmers, Labourers on the Margins of Rural Life

Isolated, poor, and often locked into subservient roles (the majority being women and children), such persons must go on coping day-by-day, year-by-year. Mutual aid has weakened, and in some zones is completely dead.

To build social movements from such starting points is a long march. State-initiated measures such as the proto-cooperatives *(Associações)* and branches of the National Peasant Association (UNACA), may provide a means of engaging some farmers, especially the better-off. Organizations to defend the interests of the rural labourer are not even on the horizon.

Traditional Authority: Between Two Stools

"I used to have many houses and goats, sheep, chickens, ducks, pigs and cattle." The old *Soba* of N'harea in Bie Province, counts his losses. "Now I live in one little room, no longer with my land and possessions."

His losses are not purely material. The *Soba* has been robbed of his standing in the community. "People used to come and talk to me, and give me a bit of money for my counsel. But now no one has any resources, and no one comes to talk to me. Our life has changed so much."

The war hit his people hard. "In 1982 it began to get worse. We had to abandon our houses and hide in the bush, even up to six times in a week. And UNITA would keep changing the time of their attacks, so we had to be ready to run at all times. When we returned to our homes, we found our things had been stolen. Later we were not free to move from our homes to cultivate our fields or to get water because of the landmines planted around the area. Our schools kept going. And sometimes we got supplies from an airlift. But we were demoralized."

"Finally in 1988, we could no longer live in N'harea. So over a period of months, we all left, about 5,000 people in all. Everyone walked. We spent days on the way, until we reached Kuito (about 120 kilometres distance) and safety."

Sanctuary at Kuito, the provincial capital, meant dependence on family networks, but also on occasional food supplies and other help from the government social agency, SEAS. The chief and many of his people were still living at Kuito in early 1992, together with 8,500 other people more recently registered there as displaced persons.

Despite this ordeal and all the losses, an ambivalence remains. The old *Soba* works the state system for help for his people. But he also still consults UNITA about his future moves: "After the ceasefire, at a UNITA rally, I asked the local UNITA representative if we could return to N'harea," the chief said. "But I was told that it was too early."

Workers in Informal Branches of the Economy

Petty traders, artisans, and day-labourers eke out livelihoods at the high-risk and low-wage ends of the market, where unstable local trade, unregulated bosses and the threat of dismissal rule. Joining their ranks every day are young men (some just demobilized) and women with few skills and no experience except wartime hustling.

Where organizations arise from these strata, they will tend to be for illicit and illegal purposes, including protection rackets.

Youth

"Angolan youth, especially those born beginning in 1972, are marked by violence and a lack of hope and confidence in the future." This Angolan social scientist's view, presented at a conference late in 1991, is a plain truth.[14]

Youth are a weakened and demoralized starting-point for civil society. This gap is all the more serious because it concerns a quarter of Angola's population. As part of a "lost generation" of the war years, most young people in the 1990s will have had only minimal formal schooling or none at all. Almost all face dismal job prospects.

Like the youthful hero of *Patriots*, an autobiographical novel by an ex-UNITA fighter, they have two ways of escaping poverty: "crime and education. The latter was not easy; the former was tempting and profitable."[15]

Not only can many young people never help to build civil society, but some seem actively destined to undermine it. For them, a slide into marginality seems inevitable.

Of course, to write off all young people from public affairs would be a mistake. Some have begun organizing spontaneously, sometimes sparked by the appalling urban environments in which they live. In Luanda's poor neighbourhoods in 1991, for example, the Youth Club of the Friends of the Bairro Rangel began to do clean-up and social projects. The Ecological Youth Group of Maianga took on tree-planting and neighbourhood flower beds. The Friends of the Environment of Ngola-Kiluanje started a community park made on the site of a rubbish-tip. The Youth League of Marcal embarked on socio-cultural activities.[16]

Can such enthusiasm be maintained? If such groupings stay independent of more powerful bodies wishing to lay claim to youth for political purposes, the answer may be yes. After all, if young people refuse to remain passive amidst the misery of Luanda's shantytowns, they could hardly be daunted by anything bigger.

Women

During the war, women were "the ones who stayed behind" in the rural homesteads, in the huts of the displaced persons' camps and in the shacks on the cities' edges. Active soldiering, or avoidance of it, was what men did. The basic jobs of sustaining others fell to women, usually from their early teens onwards. Today the female-headed household is commonplace.

Women also stayed behind in the social and economic sense. An Angolan woman living to the end of her child-bearing years can expect to deliver six or seven babies -- a rate which has not changed in 30 years. Women die from pregnancy-related causes at rates well above those of comparable countries.[17] The reasons are bound up with women's and girls' traditional roles in the household: they work longer hours and they eat poorly.

Even with some post-independence gains, rates of literacy, school enrolment and completion of primary school were lower for females than for males -- although most school participation rates were higher than similar countries such as Mozambique and Malawi.[18]

Despite these handicaps, women are an active force, mainly in the agrarian and commercial branches of the informal economy. In urban settings, where some women have begun to accumulate money and goods on their own, the ground rules in relations between the sexes may be shifting in women's favour.

Entrance into the formal sector has gone less smoothly. Only about three percent of managerial and policy-making positions in the government, and 15 percent of the seats in National and Provincial Assemblies, were filled by women.

Laws passed in the 1980s grant equal rights to women, in matters of employment, the household, inheritance and public life. These progressive statutes read well, and have raised Angola's prestige abroad. Actually enforced, however, they add up to something far less than emancipation for ordinary Angolan women. Customary practice and conventional notions of development (e.g.,"girls don't really belong in vocational training programmes") are deeply rooted, and enjoy considerable support, among both men and women.

Nevertheless, gender relations in professional and managerial strata, at least, as well as every household's need for more income, have set the stage for major legal advances.

Pressing for many changes has been the MPLA's Organization of Angolan Women (OMA). It functioned as a pressure group within the ruling party, and often had impact, such as lobbying for a progressive Family Code, eventually adopted in 1990.

Because it was always dependent politically and financially on the MPLA since its founding in 1961, and had never addressed its shortcomings in skills and internal management, the OMA's weaknesses and shallow roots among ordinary Angolan women now put its future in jeopardy. Throughout the war years, it was more a place for ritual gestures than a vehicle for creating the force that women could become in Angolan life if they were mobilized.

Having been cut loose from the MPLA in mid-1991, it faces the future in a crisis of identity and even perhaps of survival.

Meanwhile, women in professions and businesses are organizing their own associations. The revival of worker activism offers new outlooks as well.

Weak but Audible: Trade Unions, Intellectuals, NGOs

The heart, brains, and lungs of the MPLA were to have been drawn from the ranks of organized wage-earners and intellectuals. Rapid improvement in their working conditions and prestige in the heady early independence years appeared to confirm their prospects.

Sixteen years later, the falling-out is nearly total. The cozy intimacy of the early years has been lost.

Trade Unions

Everyone in a formal sector job is obliged to pay union dues to a branch of UNTA *(União Nacional dos Trabalhadores Angolanos)*, the only trade union federation permitted under law. But as UNTA's leadership noted in April 1992, it had always been a union for participating -- going along with what government wanted -- but not a union for pressing claims on behalf of members.

A year earlier, members of the food, trade and hotel industry unions had demanded that UNTA be dissolved because of its inability to defend workers' interests.

Meanwhile, as purchasing power began dropping and special privileges fell away, frustration and anger rose among all wage-earners. It burst out in a series of strikes, all unauthorized. The most serious of these hit the ports of Luanda and Namibe, Cabinda-Gulf Oil Company, and the Angolan Diamond Company, Endiama. Hospitals, schools, the national university, air traffic control towers, and even a military garage saw staff stayaways. More than 100 strikes took place across Angola in the year following the cease-fire.

In most cases, the companies and government reached settlements with workers but in 1992 the wave of strikes and job actions showed no sign of diminishing. Rattled by this labour militancy, the government proposed a new trade union law in April, 1992 which came under intense fire for its apparent lack of democracy.

Out of all this surge of collective action, however, only one new, independent union emerged by mid-1992 -- and that from among workers who had not gone on strike: journalists. Was it to be the first of many? The signals were mixed. One analyst summed up the prospects this way: "There won't be many new unions, but there will be strikes for a while to come. Don't expect much real political clout to develop through organizations of wage-earners. That's a long way off yet."

Intellectuals

Long sidelined, but not silenced, only a few of Angola's intellectuals were swept into Angola's new party politics. Most preferred to wait and see.

More interesting for many intellectuals are the political and concrete opportunities opening in media and publishing. The emergence of *Correio da Semana* ("Weekly Post") offered a new forum and focus for writers and commentators interested in provoking debate. Major figures from all parts of the political spectrum were subjected to public scrutiny of a kind never seen before in Angola's press.

The crisis in Angola's university, which erupted in a series of strikes, appeared chronic, as erosion of living and working conditions continued. A "life of the mind" was hard to sustain when there was no water for weeks on end.

Nevertheless, intellectuals showed many signs of clinging firmly to their positions of potential influence. Audible they will remain, but how wide and how deep their influence will become is still an open question.

Development NGOs

Work in support of farmers, displaced persons, and shanty-dwellers had been the monopoly of government or party agencies nearly to the end of the 1980s. With the exception of activities under the wing of church organizations -- notably Caritas Angola, the Angolan Council of Evangelical Churches, the Association of Evangelicals of Angola and the YMCA -- indigenous non-governmental organizations were never encouraged.

In Zambia, Zimbabwe and Namibia during and following their political transitions, dozens of such groups had emerged. In South Africa, there were hundreds of foreign-funded NGOs. But, in Angola such things were objects of anxiety and suspicion.

It was not wholly surprising then, that when Angola's first non-church NGO, Angolan Action for Development *(Acção Angolana para o Desenvolvimento--AAD)* announced its formation in November 1989, its main patrons were drawn from the top of the MPLA political hierarchy. With the support of German and other northern donors, AAD became a large and many-sided relief agency. Its fleet of trucks dwarfed the fleets of some branches of the state. As such, it is a highly successful case of Angolan collaboration with Northern donors to channel resources massively to victims of war and economic distress.

Other initiatives began surfacing, some with a vocation in relief and others looking toward the slow, risky work of development at community level. Among the most promising of these is Action for Rural Development and the Environment *(Acção parao Desenvolvimento Rural e Ambiente - ADRA)*, a grouping of seasoned policy-makers and technical workers in rural development. ADRA aims to focus on supporting local development initiatives through advice and brokerage services for funds and expertise.

In the provinces, concerns to revive and develop towns and regions prompted the founding of dozens of local development associations. Some examples were: the "Friends of Nambuangongo", "Friends of Damba/Uige", "Association of Natives and Friends of Libolo", the "Association of Support and Development of the East of Angola", and the "Friends of Kwanza Norte". How closed or open such societies were, how broadly and deeply rooted in their communities, how much they were motivated by public spiritedness and how much by desires to attract the donor dollar -- such questions were in the balance as local groupings multiplied by the month.

By 1991 the number of Angolan NGOs had grown to the point of establishing not one but two networks: FONGA *(Forum das ONGs Angolanas)* and CONGA *(Comité das Organizações Não-governamentais em Angola)*, the latter also including foreign non-governmental agencies.

For relief and development NGOs, as well as community-based organizations, there were many uncertainties and risks ahead. Dependence on, and competition for, external funds; domination by elites seeking new points of political leverage or just a safe haven as jobs became scarcer; increasing politicization as political parties sought tactical alliances and means of developing patronage networks; marginalization in policy debates on issues of poverty and development -- these were some of the dangers lurking as NGOs cut their own pathways through the uncharted bushlands of Angolan civil society.

Strong and Audible: Churches and Business

In Angola's new civil society, two groupings looked certain to become the heavyweights: churches and business people. They have the membership, the momentum and the support abroad.

Churches

As noted earlier, churches have been on a growth path for years. Congregations have expanded steadily and churches are packed with worshippers. Catholic seminaries are full of postulants and religious orders have many novices, especially young women.

According to Methodist Bishop Emílio de Carvalho "the church in Angola is the fastest-growing in Africa, if not in the world. My own church gets seven percent more members every year. Every year we name 25 to 30 new pastors, a rate of 10 percent. We sometimes found 10 new congregations per year."[19]

Bishop Carvalho's church has enjoyed good relations with the MPLA. Indeed it counts among its adherents a number of top government leaders. The Methodist church in Luanda is, according to local wits, "the MPLA leadership at prayer."

The Angolan Council of Protestant Churches (CAIE) comprises at least 12 churches and their nearly half-million members. Other Protestant-linked churches, including those adhering to indigenous African beliefs, account for more than half a million members.

Larger yet, is the Roman Catholic Church, the religious home of 40 to 45 percent of the Angolan population. Altogether, at least half of all adult Angolans would consider themselves Christians.

Believers outnumber members of all political parties by a wide margin. The National Directorate of Religious Affairs oversees the process (created by law only in 1987) by which church groups gain official recognition. Once registered, churches became eligible for subsidies and special access to goods and services. The government has had to move cautiously, and keep a sharp eye out for frauds and opportunists looking for ways to tap state resources. As of 1992 only 22 denominations enjoyed such status, although the government, itself, estimates that more than 100 exist.[20] Recognized or unrecognized, Angolan churches go right on proselytizing and organizing.

Given such a massive and committed following, it is little wonder that some church leaders, after years in the political wilderness, are now being warmly welcomed.

The six-day visit by Pope John Paul II in June 1992 and his welcome by all political parties is a sign of the importance with which the Catholic church is taken in the run-up to elections.

Hundreds of thousands of votes could hang on a single utterance from some church leaders. That is why, perhaps, church pronouncements in the prelude to Angola's first multi-party elections were careful and muted.

Political leaders look not only to what churches can deliver politically, but also as a means to bridge the enormous gaps in education, health care and welfare services. At independence, the state took up such tasks, seeing them as obligations to the citizenry and to development imperatives. Now the state is under pressure from the IMF and World Bank to shed them.

Some church leaders hesitate to seize this cup of friendship proffered by the state. For they sense it is a poisoned chalice -- a burden far exceeding the capacity of any group in civil society to take on. It is also one which many Angolans within, and outside, the churches feel is properly the role of the collective, public institutions.

Thus the churches are under many new and unaccustomed pressures as leading actors in civil society. They can also apply their considerable powers to put pressure on others. How they will exercise those powers as an elected government gets down to business will be one of the most closely-watched aspects of post-election Angola.

Business Interests

Business and professional associations, long kept alive in informal private networks, went formal and moved into the spotlight once political "decompression" began. The market system had come out of the closet, after all, so the time for businessmen and women to regain their self-respect was at hand. Professionals also moved to amplify their voices. Everyone started to get organized.

Truckers, hotel-keepers, vehicle sales agents, taxi-drivers, teachers, doctors, lawyers, and translators -- many types of entrepreneurs and professional workers -- formed associations in 1990 and 1991 and their numbers kept growing. Some were regional in scope, such as the Agro-Industrial and Commercial Association, based in Lubango, and the Commercial and Industrial Association of Luanda. Alongside these, there appeared strong branches for women such as the Women Entrepreneurs Association of Huila *(Associação das Mulheres Empresárias da Huila)*. Others aimed for national prominence, such as the Angolan Industrial Association.

Regaining self-respect was, of course, one of their less compelling motivations. The *patrões* (bosses, owners) were organizing to influence the political climate, and the laws of the land. Through seminars, lunches, assemblies and tours, they were refining the consensus among members on such key issues as labour regulations, taxes and access to foreign exchange. Politicians and policy-makers were brought along.

Angolan business circles also lost little time building links with kindred organizations in Portugal and elsewhere. Out of that work emerged yet other formal institutions, such as the Portugal/Angola Chamber of Commerce and Industry.

In such Angolan magazines as *Comércio Externo* (External Commerce) the *patrões* tried to allay fears among wage-earners, and to put across their message that the "new" emerging social class would bring the prosperity to Angola that the centralized economy had failed to do.

In their policy statements to government, they have made clear their wishes about the political influence and support they require from government to get on with the job of generating wealth. In an editorial appealing for peace, *Comércio Externo* showed no hesitation in speaking on behalf of civil society when it wrote, "Civil society is ready to support more sacrifices, necessary in the phase of reconstruction in which we live."[21]

Others in civil society would agree with the business press that nothing of value can happen unless peace is guaranteed. When it comes to the degree of readiness to support more sacrifices, and just who would share those sacrifices, the *patrões* are unlikely to find much common ground with their compatriots in Angolan civil society. The debates about Angola's future -- where, for instance, the peace dividend should go -- have yet to begin in earnest.

8 | The Peace Dividend and the Problem of Poverty

"When will all this 'independence' come to an end?" A plaintive question, posed by a woman in a displaced persons' settlement in Kwanza Sul Province in 1985, reveals the frustration and bewilderment of many Angolans after years of war and economic decline.[1] For them, "independence" has meant the opposite of what was expected: not plenty but penury, not contentment but misery.

With the war at an end, hope is rising that old wrongs and deprivations may finally be redressed. If that happens, "independence" may then regain its former meaning of freedom from want and humiliation. Unfortunately, there are ominous signs that the 1990s will see little reduction in poverty, rather its spread and increasing intensity.

The official end of hostilities does, however, bring hope. War was an abyss into which Angola's human and financial resources disappeared for 16 years. With growing voracity each year, it swallowed up to half the national budget (21 percent of the GDP). It forced government to spend far beyond its revenues. Such spending in proportion to national income was matched only in some Middle Eastern countries, where military establishments are enormous.

The difference between what the war consumed and what the military requires in the postwar period should equal the Peace Dividend. How much will this improve the lives of the country's deprived majority? That is a pivotal question for Angola's future.

The peace dividend's cash value depends on the level of military spending. If this could be reduced to four percent of GDP — the average for sub-Saharan Africa — and if Angola's GDP is US$10 billion dollars, then (using the military's 1990 level of 21 percent of GDP as a benchmark) one year's peace dividend should come to US$1.7 billion. This would add about US$170 per capita in national income, per annum.

Where will the peace dividend go? The answer depends on choices made about the pace and direction of Angola's recovery, who influences those choices and how.

Deprivation

By most indices, Angolans live in absolute poverty — some of the worst living conditions in the world.

UNICEF's foremost indicator of general public well-being is the annual number of deaths of children under five.[2] In its 1992 ranking of 170 countries on this fundamental measure, Angola ranks third from the bottom, just behind Mozambique and Afghanistan, with 292 child deaths per 1,000 live births in 1990.

On the "Index of Human Suffering", prepared by the Population Crisis Committee in 1987, Angola scored 91 out of 100; only Mozambique, with 95, knew more suffering.[3] On the United Nations Development Programme's Human Development Index (HDI) — a composite measure of longevity, adult literacy, mean years of schooling, and per capita GDP adjusted for real purchasing power — Angola ranks 147th in a list of 160 countries based on data from the late 1980s.

In the same study, Angola was first in the world for the gap between its low HDI score and its "middle income" ranking by GNP per capita. Angola lags behind all other countries in translating its wealth into improvements in the lives of its people, largely due to the war.[4]

There are no data on *distribution* of income, knowledge and chance of survival beyond four years of age in Angola, but data from comparable countries, and other evidence, suggest a society of gross inequality in world terms.

Statistics which locate Angolans at the bottom of world tables could be cited at length. These statistics may also distort matters. Is the "average" Brazilian five times better off than the "average" Angolan? Such a conclusion could be drawn from a comparison of indices. Grossly skewed income distribution in both Brazil and Angola creates a fallacious average. Hence one can ask how much we actually learn from such indices. Beyond the numbers, however, are what Angolans themselves say.

They know full well that they are deprived, both in relative and absolute terms. To a researcher, journalist or visiting politician, Angolans in the rural areas or city shantytowns speak clearly of their frustrations and their needs: to feed and clothe themselves and their families; to have clean water close at hand; to see their children grow up healthy and get a better chance in life; to be assured of medical services; to gain access to land and the means to earn a livelihood and to house themselves.

The wants of poor Angolans are the same as those of people the world over — they want to satisfy basic needs. And those needs in Angola are very basic indeed.

Obstacles

What gives such basic needs special urgency and force in Angola is the depth and duration of the goods famine and general dispossession. Especially for rural dwellers, the means to produce, and the incentives to make a living, have been constantly in short supply. Why have basic needs not been met?

Several explanations are advanced at a broad level. One of them (by theorists sympathetic to socialism) assigns blame for chronic shortages to the logic or laws of motion of the state socialist model — the one used to revamp Angola's economy in the 1970s.

The result in Angola was like that observed elsewhere: a "resource-constrained economy" whose main feature is "the continuous reproduction of shortages."[5] Managers were forced by central planning to scramble for inputs, and lose sight of end users and their needs. Thus they could never deliver the goods in the right amounts at the right times.

The shallow pool of skilled people, especially managers, was a more important reason. Portuguese colonial rule had denied schooling, and a chance at salaried jobs, to Angolans. Most Portuguese settlers could barely read and write.[6] More importantly, they shouldered Angolans aside from even low-status jobs, denying them a chance at training in basic skills. Only a handful of Angolans managed to gain higher educational and technical credentials.

Finally, and most importantly, was the war which diverted precious human and material resources and choked off lines of supply, thus giving most of the economy a *coup de grâce* as it collapsed.

A New Beginning?

The war and state socialist models are now receding into the past. Basic education and training are under way. Have the main obstacles to a healthy recovery then been swept aside? Will the peace dividend flow naturally toward the fight against poverty?

As it plans a recovery and the use of the peace dividend, Angola's leadership faces competing claims on resources. These come from interested parties both inside and outside the country. Only some of them hold that acceptance or rejection of specific recovery measures should depend on their anti-poverty potential. Most of the parties argue for other criteria — such as prospective contribution to GDP growth, to export earnings, or to overall net transfers of resources to Northern economic interests. They wish to see those foreign-oriented criteria applied to remodel the economy, guide investments, and re-cast the role of the state. Reducing poverty is just one among a number of aims competing for pre-eminence.

Just how high it will eventually stand on the list of priorities depends on compromises reached among major blocs inside and outside Angola. The most important will be the compromises reached between the Angolan state and foreign interests, public and private. Also important will be compromises turning on state versus private domestic interests; military versus non-military interests; one private sector interest versus another; employers (public and private) versus organized labour or others in civil society, and so on.

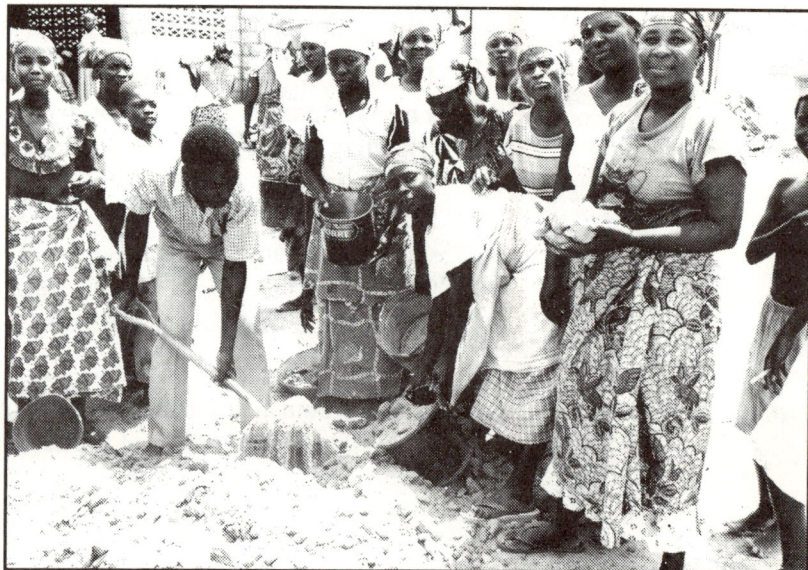

Photo 8.1: *Residents of Sambizanga shantytown, starting work on a new neighbourhood centre and clinic.*

The content of those compromises will depend on the respective clout of various interests. Above the voices of the poor calling for satisfaction of basic needs, come the cries of certain urban dwellers frustrated because they can no longer fly to Rio twice a year or import automobiles and designer clothing as they could until 1992.

Thus the obstacles to a healthy recovery and the effective use of the peace dividend have by no means been swept aside.

The Social Pyramid and the New Poor

In its economic review of Angola, the World Bank offers a thumbnail sketch of the country's main social categories in the closing years of the Portuguese rule pre-1975:

- A dominant class of absentee owners, resident mainly in Europe;

- Senior business people, mainly Portuguese administrators and military officers, resident in Angola to manage its affairs;

- A lower middle class of small proprietors, salaried employees and petty officials, virtually all Portuguese;

- An urban proletariat, composed of both Portuguese and Angolans; and a rural proletariat, entirely black, with lower wages than the urban proletariat;

- A "lumpen proletariat" in the urban areas.[7]

If Angola's rural majority were added (it is not clear why the World Bank omitted them), the sketch would be complete in its essentials. In the intervening 20 years, some categories have grown and others declined. The number of foreigners radically diminished, but the basic structure was preserved.

What then changed? After 1975, the proletariat (category 4), especially in the countryside, shrank considerably; the small proprietors also shrank, but did not disappear since Angolan traders replaced the departing Portuguese to some extent. In Kwanza Sul province, for example, there were about 3,000 "bush traders" in the colonial period; by 1991 there were only about 300.[8]

What grew in numbers and power was the category of administrators, officers and managers. This new "state class", with chains of clients among state employees as well as actors in the formal and informal branches of the private economy, consolidated its position at the top of the pyramid.

The absentee stratum identified by the World Bank shed many members as Portuguese holding companies lost their assets, but it also gained even more powerful new members, especially in the oil and diamond businesses and banks. The absentees have local representatives and clients.

Finally, the category of the urban poor, which the World Bank terms a "lumpen proletariat", is now massive. Traditional farmers and other non-wage-earning rural workers have, meanwhile, declined as a proportion of the population. The World Bank estimates that rural members of the economically active population dropped from 74 percent in 1970 to 37 percent by 1985.[9]

The Non-Poor and Power

What does all this signify for Angola's recovery and the use of the peace dividend? Among other things, it suggests that poverty has diversified and expanded, especially on the edges of cities. It no longer has one, but several centres of gravity. If the problem of poverty is to be tackled effectively, several points of leverage and several approaches to it must be found.

The ways in which poverty is reproduced have shifted. Political and economic factors, always important, now loom even larger above such things as technology or climate. Approaches based on technical "modernization" alone are clearly not viable. If the power and distribution questions are ignored, technical modernization may well make matters worse.

Today's non-poor are mainly Angolans, not Portuguese. If, however, their income and security are met mainly by exports from enclaves, or the import of luxury automobiles and foods, almost the only things about poverty disturbing them is the high rate of crime — for which the easy answer is private security systems. Some may gain nothing (or even stand to lose) from a concerted effort to end poverty.

On the other hand, an Angolan whose income and security depends on sales of cheap footwear, clothing and foodstuffs to a mass market may take a different point of view on anti-poverty policies.

Which of those two archetypes of the non-poor will gain an upper hand in Angolan politics depends on the pace and direction of Angola's economic development.

This last point is crucial in advancing a recovery programme. The World Bank says, choosing its words carefully: "The non-poor are usually politically powerful, and they exert a strong influence on policy. It is important to design poverty-reducing policies that will be supported, or at least not actively resisted, by the non-poor."[10]

Debates

Angola's recovery, and the use of the peace dividend, are being conditioned by social structures shaped by two violent, poverty-creating historical epochs: colonial rule and post-colonial war. There was a sharp break between the two. As Angola enters another epoch, a second sharp break is at hand.

In a number of policy areas there are strong tensions. Major choices remain to be made, and new opportunities seized.

City *versus* Countryside

The already-wide gulf between the city and countryside became a gaping chasm during the war years. Whether measured by the numbers of traditional farmers in the MPLA (less than two percent of members in 1981); or the countryside's share of all merchandise sold through state channels (36 percent of total value in 1984); or the population served by medical units (26,000 persons per health unit *outside* provincial capitals versus 6,000 *in* provincial capitals), Angolans in rural areas have gotten the poorer deal.

Some rural Angolans resolved this simply by moving to where the benefits were (Chapter One). They also took up new livelihoods, linking cities and hinterlands, usually out of sight of the authorities. Urban-rural trade systems are still poorly known.

Most Angolan farmers are from the central highlands, where UNITA's following is especially strong. Add to that, the mining of pathways and fields, loss of crops, cattle, houses and mobility, conscription and obligatory shifting of homesteads, and the basis for anger and estrangement is all the more apparent. As an Angolan researcher on rural issues put it: "There is great resentment, something undefinable but deep among the peasants. The peasants say, 'the government does nothing for us, worse yet, it exploits us'."[12]

The farmers' response was a common, and costly, one — withdrawal and non-co-operation. Some joined the ranks of UNITA, while others passively aided the guerrillas. The flow of food and fibre to the cities and factories became a trickle, especially through official channels.

State marketing agents were thought to get only about five percent of Angola's maize output each year. Hence the plaintive remark of the Angolan Minister of Industry in February 1992 that to keep industries going, the state spends US$ 35 million each year to import maize, cotton, sunflower and other raw materials — products which Angola used to export in large amounts.[12]

Angolan experts in rural development are calling for a fundamental change of approach. Their arguments point not toward the mere restoration of things as they were in the colonial era, in which well-endowed private estates encroached on the lands and livelihoods of impoverished small farmers. Rather, they argue for a re-appreciation of rural life as a whole. They propose:

- Among those responsible for designing and implementing rural development policies, there must come a much deeper basis in facts and understanding of the realities of rural life (systems of production and marketing, indigenous practices) and the transformations which war and economic decline have brought about there (population movements, parallel commerce, new labour shortages);

- Rural dwellers must be allowed to participate in and ultimately control their own development actions, designed in terms meaningful to them. They must be encouraged to build their own organized means to articulate and defend their interests as producers, consumers and citizens;

- A new role is needed for the state, one which is supportive rather than directive. It must give full scope to the creative capacities and initiatives of rural people. It should recognize the depth and validity of their local knowledge of crops, soils, water management, livestock and artisanal production. Finally it must combine modern scientific research with indigenous knowledge for concrete improvements in rural lives and livelihoods;

- At a broader level, macro-economic policies must be jettisoned which give privileged status to projects of "babylonian" dimensions but inhibit development by small scale producers. Instead, policies need to be developed which put producer goods, transport and marketing services, and incentive goods at the disposal of small scale producers.[13]

However, since a large proportion of poor Angolans now live on the margins of large towns and cities, an approach to poverty is no longer chiefly a matter of rural development. Policies providing food at low cost to vulnerable people, for example, may merit continuation on anti- poverty grounds, even if they favour urban consumers and could penalize those farmers capable of producing surpluses. Tough choices also arise around investments: sewers and drains in the cities and roads and bridges in the countryside may both be justified on anti-poverty grounds.

Rural dwellers, in principle, may have the space to organize, but gaining leverage is another thing. As long as petroleum and other mineral-based enclaves remain the exclusive engines of Angola's accumulation, rural producers will be sidelined. More than exploitation, a greater risk is that of neglect and marginalization from Angola's economic and social mainstream. People in rural zones will have to press hard for their place in the economy.

Investment *versus* **Consumption**

State socialist regimes are commonly charged with "investment bias" — of plowing back too much of current income and squeezing wage-earners' consumption to just the minimum needed to keep body and soul together.

In Angola's case, the charge is different: both investment and consumption were poor. The World Bank says: "In sum, it can be concluded that out of Angola's oil income little was returned to taxpayers or saved for the future."[14]

The Angolan leadership is now being pressed to adopt a new "investment bias" from an opposite ideological perspective and another generation of Angolans is being asked to tighten its belt for a better future, guaranteed this time not by the immutable laws of scientific socialism but by the invisible hand of free enterprise.

The investment-consumption trade-off comes down to how much improvement in current living standards consumers can postpone, and for how long. The value people place on future, as against present, consumption is a subjective and sensitive thing. Given current basic needs of the majority, and the "needs" created by exposure to the conspicuous consumption of a minority, most Angolans no doubt have difficulty postponing consumption. The big questions are, of course: whose living standards will be improved through holding down whose current consumption?

Post-revolutionary Angola already has a track record of trying to generate future income, and putting a lid on consumption.

In the lull that followed the 1975-1976 hostilities, the government launched a recovery programme. For private and public sector alike it was a time of investment. The leadership struck deals with the enclave companies in petroleum and diamonds to permit them to take home profits or to invest according to their wishes. For other businesses, the government made foreign investment attractive through generous terms on repatriating profits.

The state put much of its own hard currency into the badly crippled transport sector, repairing roads and bridges and importing 11,000 vehicles, mainly trucks and buses. It got most factories working again (60 percent of installed capacity was at work in 1980 versus 40 percent in 1977) and it began investing in new enterprises.

Many of these were, however, foreign contractor "turnkey" projects in which all equipment and know-how were shipped in from abroad, set up by foreigners and then handed over, with the keys, to Angolans. Beef ranches, pineapple plantations, factories for fancy shoes — such projects looked good in the sales agent's glossy descriptions, but they were of dubious viability.

In the end, this early investment push came to almost nothing. Plant and equipment were destroyed or paralyzed by lack of energy and raw materials as the war flared up again in the 1980s. Poor management and maintenance put much of the rest out of action.

At first, controlling consumption was not so difficult. In the countryside, austerity quickly became an outright goods famine. The flow of things rural people wanted to buy — clothes, salt, sugar, tools, blankets, soap — dried up. The purchasing power of the kwanza in the hands of farmers evaporated and they stopped selling to the state, whose low farmgate prices paid for produce and livestock soon became a subject of pointed jokes.

Holding down consumption by city dwellers and those in the state sector proved more difficult. For those civil servants connected to the state's export and import companies, or richer Angolans connected with the right people in the state and party apparatuses, consumption knew few limits. As one observer noted in 1987, "Consumerism has jumped the patch-and-make-good stage to reach the throw-away culture in one move."[15] In the late 1980s Angola paid out nearly US$250 million per year for official travel abroad — almost as much as for imports of food and raw materials for industry.[16]

The rise of powerful social groupings now put special twists on the investment-consumption dynamic.

First come those with basic needs. The war pushed hundreds of thousands of people, formerly net producers, into situations where they could only be net consumers. Farmers became landless, displaced people hustling for a living on the edge of the cities; healthy young people became cripples; some of the old and the young, abandoned by their families, became wards of the state; many young men became skilled at handling firearms, using those skills for armed robbery.

Second, there is a well-entrenched privileged group in the state and its companies and at the wholesale end of the parallel market. Their presence diverts resources toward not only high-status consumption (expensive cars and trips abroad) but also high-status investment (jetliners, elaborate motorways and luxury dwellings). These upwardly mobile groupings (and their children) in the cities thus stand to put substantial claims on national income.

Third, tension between privileged and non-privileged generates its own pressures to spend on activities of doubtful productivity. For example, demands to strengthen police forces, public or private, are already intense.

Angola's new government will face a swirling vortex generated by these types of tensions. It will have to strike balances among many competing, long-term claims. Added to these will be the claims of foreign creditors. In short, its freedom of manoeuvre is going to be limited.

It is possible, however, that the leadership can work its way free of these tensions to decide in favour of one type of investment which theory and practice around the world have shown to pay enormous returns. That is investment in human beings, at basic levels.

Water supply, sanitation, primary and adult education for numeracy, literacy and other basic skills, preventive primary health care systems — these are investments which, whenever they have seen them, Angolans welcome.

Beyond the *what* issue is the *how* issue. Here the processes by which investment decisions are reached, and the degree of control by people over the stream of benefits from those decisions, will be crucial to their success. Angolans are waiting not just to *take* whatever a state may offer, but to *take part* as full actors in development processes.

Generating Jobs *versus* Pushing up Productivity

As Chapter Three showed, Angolans do not lack energy and resourcefulness in developing livelihoods for themselves. At the levels of the neighbourhood and small town especially, they find niches and create jobs.

In the period 1976-1979 the state became the nation's main employer as it took over plantations, farms and factories. It put thousands to work as teachers. It showed special energy in creating positions in its administrative sectors.

Since 1987, the government has been promising to cut jobs in the state companies and public service. In 1990, President dos Santos hinted that 70,000 jobs out of 120,000 would be cut from state payrolls. In fact, the state began shedding labour in the early 1980s, mainly in the countryside. The state coffee authority cut its plantation workforce from 40,000 in 1982 to 19,700 in 1989. The government shed tens of thousands of labourers from the payrolls of state farms in the mid-1980s, sometimes by merely re-modelling them as co-operatives. Private firms also retrenched workers.

Mass lay-offs are nothing new in Angola. But the 1990s will see them occur on an even greater scale, and this time in the cities. As many as 160,000, or about one-fifth of the non-military labour force may be struck from payrolls. Added to this labour force are about 120,000 officially and spontaneously demobilized combatants pouring onto the market for jobs in 1992.

Recent Oxford University studies on poverty in Luanda, commissioned by UNICEF, suggest that these retrenchments will hit state sector workers hard. The households of 35 to 40 percent of these employees were, in early 1990, already below the poverty line. State employment has always been crucial to Luanda's economy, with about 37 percent of all households dependent on it.

Unemployment in Luanda is high. About 26 percent of those surveyed had no job at all and the jobless in 1990/91 accounted for only about a third of the poor. To unemployment must be added a large percentage of under-employment: the working poor in jobs that pay very little.[17]

Returns to labour in the countryside have been even lower. So, too, are benefits of collective consumption, such as water, health, transport and schooling services. However, the depth of poverty and its distribution across the country are not known in nearly the same detail as in Luanda.

Employment with decent income is a fundamental challenge to Angola's recovery. Angolans already work hard for meagre returns and they are ready to work even harder and produce even more — but only if certain conditions are met: Enough to eat and maintain their health; availability of the tools, materials and services allowing them to apply their labour and to deliver their products (that is, everything from hoes to bus services to improved skills); and incentives in terms of good prices and wages, backed by real goods and services.

The upward economic spiral, however, in which city and countryside, formal and informal sectors, are linked dynamically, is unlikely to take off if the mass of Angolans are pressed further into poverty. If the distribution of income becomes even more skewed than it already is, recovery is improbable. The Oxford study for UNICEF makes this point directly:

"If the benefits of rural or urban growth are narrowly based, the lack of demand that results (will) not allow rural or urban entrepreneurs to expand to benefit from new technology and from economies of scale, or for new complementary economic activities to emerge and develop."[18]

It is one thing to celebrate the virtues of the free market and informal sector, but another to develop the policies which will promote the demand which will generate sustainable employment.

Job creation based on wholesale "informalization" is a questionable strategy. It raises the spectre of ever-expanding masses of poor people scrambling for places in a stagnant, low-income market. The formal sector, including state-financed activities, will remain the engine of the economy. Informal activities tend to flourish or decline with it.

However, given the conditions of grave vulnerability among key groups — young people, women and war-affected — support to the informal sector merits creative, targeted policy and action to generate jobs. Experience elsewhere suggests that special programmes are best targeted on individuals in such key groups rather than on enterprises as such, where owners would reap the benefits. Macro policies that promote basic goods over luxury items can also multiply jobs.

Two growth paths suggest themselves as means of absorbing large amounts of unskilled and semi-skilled labour:

First, rural production: crop, livestock, fish, and forest products.

Second, construction: roads, bridges, houses, irrigation works, and land reclamation.

For growth to develop along these paths, macro policies will have to be matched by programme initiatives. A basic principle would then be to let the workforce employ capital (tools, materials, energy — including food) rather than the other way around. Human capacities ("human capital") would be central, with training in basic skills, administration and the organization of work.

Outward Orientation *versus* Greater Self-Sufficiency

As in most countries on the periphery of the world's economic power blocs, Angola's economy is locked into the international system. Some form of engagement with that system is inevitable. Disengagement and autarchy of a kind seen in China from 1945 to the 1970s (with many positive results) is not possible for a country of Angola's small population and low skill levels. In coming to terms with this imperative to engage, the key word is *terms*: For what purposes, to whose benefit and to what degree should Angola's economy be outwardly-oriented? In what directions should it go — entirely toward the North where its current trade and investment partners come from, or increasingly towards other countries in the South?

Such issues have yet to generate wide debate in Angola, but they are cropping up with increasing frequency in discussions among intellectuals and church leaders. Concerns have been voiced, for example, about the return of foreigners to claim abandoned property, and the close ties with, and apparently increasing dependence on, transnational corporations including big banks.

Set against moribund internal industry and a distorted service sector, neither of which is strongly oriented towards fulfilling basic needs, the picture is even more worrisome.

Angolans raising these kinds of doubts have reason to be worried. For the economic model of export-dominated growth, which big private and multilateral banks advocate with an evangelical zeal, is the subject of increasing criticism from policy-makers and economists who have reviewed the histories of many nations' development in this century.

Their findings support the idea that soundly-based development concentrates inwardly on building a national market and a skilled workforce; exports supplement this to buy capital goods. Later, greater emphasis on exports, based selectively on strengths built up during the inward phase, becomes possible.

Especially where it rests on enclaves or one or two primary products, export-led approaches tend not to bring development, but lop-sided growth — at least in the absence of a strong state to plow back the benefits of an outward orientation in ways that promote a healthier, better-skilled population for whom the playing fields are level.

With its high, and rising, export earnings from oil, Angola has more room to manoeuvre. *If* world oil prices rise to US$25 per barrel, and output rises by 50 percent over 1991 levels, Angola could become sub-Saharan Africa's third largest earner of foreign exchange after Nigeria and South Africa by 1995 — with a population one-quarter that of South Africa and one-ninth that of Nigeria.

It faces a margin of choice that few other African countries know, and can plow its petroleum earnings back into a national economy over which Angolans retain control, and from which all Angolans may benefit. The compelling need to put more resources into export activities (and into non-productive imports) is not at all apparent.

If, as has been reported, projected Angolan oil production for the period up to about 1995 was already sold in 1991 and 1992 on the futures market in order to solve cash-flow problems of 1992, then Angola may face more, not fewer, financial constraints.[19] Its ability to meet claims of the poor and war-affected, *and* its ability to negotiate with powerful outsiders, will be compromised.

Foreign loans will then loom even larger in Angola's recovery. This in turn could limit Angolan abilities to cope flexibly and creatively with pressures to overhaul its economy. Indeed the imperatives of the nation's foreign debt already hang heavily on Angolans — including some not yet born. That debt is a main point of leverage for powerful institutions, and their internal allies, to force a further outward orientation on Angola's economy and society.

Structural Adjustment and its Discontents

Falling standards of living and diminishing public control over the economy have long been acknowledged, especially by Angolans themselves. Economic health and political standing — the two inter-connected imperatives of accumulation and legitimation — were increasingly at stake as war and mismanagement took their toll.

As early as 1982, in the face of a drop in world oil prices and a resurgence of South African and guerrilla action, the Angolan leadership began the first of what was to become a number of efforts at economic adjustment. A series of emergency plans transpired from government offices:

- In February 1983 the *Plano Global da Emergência (PGE)* (Global Emergency Plan) was launched;

- In August 1987 there followed the *Programa de Saneamento Económico e Financeiro (SEF)* (Programme for Economic and Financial Restructuring);

- In 1989 came the *Programa de Recuperação Económica (PRE)* (Programme of Economic Recovery);

- In mid-1990 a reactivated version of the SEF, the *Programa de Acção do Governo (PAG)* (Government Action Programme).

Their basic aims were similar: scale-down large investment plans, drop loss-making enterprises, shed labour from payrolls, curb imports, reduce barriers to foreign investment, encourage rural producers — in a word, to try to stabilize an out-of-balance economy and oblige it to live within its means in time of all-out war.

Nevertheless, year after year, these programmes died. Pressures of war, competition among bureaucratic blocs and private interests inside the country and economic and political pressures from outside, all combined to block their implementation.

Only the PAG was applied comprehensively, with concrete consequences for the state and the people. Its overall aims were to revive production, stabilize finances and overhaul the economy along lines of a regulated capitalist system.

The heart of the strategy included a curb on consumption and a squeeze of the supply of money; the selling-off (or handing-back to original owners) of state property and enterprises; and the removal of price controls, thus effectively adopting the parallel market as the legal market of the land.

Implied was a further shifting of the power balance between government and private sectors: the state had to relinquish many policy instruments needed to regulate the economy on behalf of the citizenry.

Central planning, and "soft" budgets for state agencies and enterprises began coming to an end. The national currency began to undergo a series of devaluations. The New Kwanza was introduced, exchanged at par value with the old Kwanza. The currency swap was an attempt to mop up some of the 90 percent of all Angolan money circulating outside the banking system. In what seemed like confiscation to many, it gave people only five percent of their cash holdings in currency, the other 95 percent being in promissory notes — which some people could begin to redeem in 1992.

Urban consumers began to pay more of the real costs of their electricity, telephone, water, transport — including international air travel — and other public services. Some official channels of supply of food and other consumer goods began to shut their doors, with the loss to consumers of many of the entitlements inscribed on their ration card, the *cartão de abastecimento*. Subsidies on everything except cooking oil, beans, rice, sugar and infant formula were ended.

Figure 8.1: *Cartoon (Lito Silva)*

Ancestor left: "Hey, now what is that?"
Ancestor middle: "Don't you know? They say that for Angola, instead of the usual package, the IMF sent a CONTAINER!"
Ancestor right: "And just guess whose head it's going to fall on?!"

Finally, and most hesitantly in urban areas, workers on state payrolls began to be terminated.

These were unpopular, and therefore politically risky, moves. For as Angola moved toward its elections in 1992, the results of the adjustment measures were hitting people hard. Inflation for most urban households was running at an annual rate of about 150 percent. Many rural households had been made destitute in the currency swap. Returns from informal trading jobs were dropping. The introduction of school fees was mooted. Means to stem cholera outbreaks were in jeopardy, and citizens were told that they should soon expect to pay for medical care, hitherto free. Robberies were mounting. Finally, hunger was rising, blunted only by Angola's best harvest in 11 years.

Meanwhile, there were few signs of the positive results promised from the adjustment measures — stimulation of internal production to achieve a balance between supply and demand. Despite their encouraging noises about making Angola eligible for cheaper loans the IMF and World Bank had, by mid-1992, scarcely rewarded Angola for carrying out these measures.[20]

Adjustment's Uneven Impact

Before the adjustment measures were applied, the Oxford studies on poverty in Luanda had warned of their impact on food security, health and livelihoods of the poor and near-poor. The economists looked beyond the macro-economic drafting boards, where structural adjustment programmes are designed, to the meso-economic levels where the distribution of adjustment's effects among rich and poor comes into focus.

They suggested that if a broad anti-poverty component is missing from the core of a structural adjustment programme, and if special measures or "safety nets" are included in an adjustment programme only to compensate immediate victims (state workers made redundant, for example) then the net effects are almost certain to be harsh and inequitable. They projected more malnutrition, poorer health and a decline in purchasing power for broad numbers of Luanda's vulnerable households — essentially, growing poverty.

Angolan policy-makers have the late-comers' advantage in assessing structural adjustment. Most other African countries submitted to their adjustment programmes some 10 to 15 years earlier. The effects are now well known.

In the balance is the question of whether Angolan policy-makers can, or will, use these lessons to negotiate better terms with those who insist on the most severe elements of structural adjustment.

The lessons are obvious: classical adjustment programmes have signally failed to improve the lives of Africa's poor majorities. Indeed, they have usually worsened them, as even IMF and World Bank researchers seem to have admitted.[21]

Moreover, available evidence suggests that structural adjustment programmes have failed even in their own terms.

As the authors of the study of poverty in Luanda write about the structural adjustment programmes' deflationary macro-economic policies and inequitable meso-economic policies, they "have failed against criteria of both economic growth and equity (i.e., allocation of resources according to need).

"Firstly, they have failed to successfully eliminate the balance of payments and fiscal deficits for which they were designed; secondly, they have failed to promote national economic growth; thirdly, they have failed to increase rates of investment in the economy, and therefore risk compromising future long term growth."[22]

Such observations complement, and take further, earlier work by other policy and research bodies. These point toward a conclusion that structural adjustment programmes have normally gone beyond mere failure to reduce poverty: they have increased poverty, sometimes on a massive scale. One leading social scientist, in an early, and exhaustive review of the subject concluded:

"It seems correct to conclude that, overall, prevailing adjustment programmes tend to increase aggregate poverty, or in other words the number of people — and of children — living below the poverty line."[23]

From Africa, doubts were crystallized and critiques articulated at the 1988 Khartoum Conference on the Human Dimension of Africa's Economic Recovery, organized by the United Nations Economic Commission for Africa, when 50-odd research papers piled on the evidence of the failures of conventional structural adjustment programmes. The Conference's closing resolution stated, "Far too many of these structural adjustment programmes...are rending the fabric of African society. Rather than improve the human condition... [they] have aggravated it."[24]

From other quarters the critiques go even further, and sometimes gain a barbed edge, as when someone referred to the International Monetary Fund as the "Infant Mortality Foundation."[25]

Angolans face a host of doubts about the policies, in large measure not of their own choosing. Just as the war exposed their essential vulnerability to forces beyond their borders, so too do the post-war needs for loans to rebuild. Angolans who have followed recent measures with growing anxiety include the churches. A Canadian newsletter linked with Protestant churches cites the words of an Angolan churchman in 1991:

"Alberto Sambetatale emphasized that the resources of Angola must be used for the good of Angolans and 'so far, for the past 400 years, they have been used for others. People need to participate not only in producing the wealth of the country, but also share in spending it.' He adds that Angolans recognize the government had to adopt a capitalist ideology under pressure from the U.S. and as the only way to end the war. But, he says 'the new way of capitalism will probably not be good for us either, as far as economic justice is concerned. Maybe later we will be able to work out a better way for ourselves'."[26]

9

A Look Ahead

This book has reviewed some of the human dimensions of a war that some say began in 1975, others 1961. Still others argue that it all began 500 years ago with the first voyage of Columbus to the Americas, when his Portuguese counterpart Diogo Cao began sailing to the Kongo Kingdom in the northern reaches of Angola.

In the year commemorating Columbus' landfall, a bit of reflection on history gives the edge to the late 1400s as the beginning of Angola's agonies. From that time onward, Angolans have not been left in peace, nor allowed to work for themselves. Up to the mid-1800s, at gunpoint and in shackles, four million Angolans helped populate the Americas as slaves, thus giving Angola its appellation, "Mother of Nations".

Viewed as the end of a 500-year war, peace in Angola today could be seen as a kind of millennium — or at least half a millennium.

But is Angola's a sustainable peace?

Leaders of Angola's contending parties and their respective armies say that it should be. Angolans from every walk of life say that it must be. They are exhausted by war and its attendant miseries.

But the war also broke public confidence. The prolongation of the conflict and the repeated postponement of economic reforms have left Angolans with deep suspicions about the sincerity of politicians. No matter that everyone knows that foreign interests, especially those with clients on Angola's borders, had kept the cauldron of war at a boil for years. Angolans remain skeptical that their internal politics can sustain a peace and put the nation back together again.

Nevertheless, the two main parties are campaigning to win. Neither is publicly considering defeat or the role of "loyal opposition" should it suffer election defeat. Such self-conviction must be tempered by the great need for post-election national unity and reconciliation. Many Angolans sense the dangers here, thus adding to their anxieties and fear of further upheaval.

Among the politicians themselves, engaging as they do in election rhetoric, suspicions and antagonisms have come to the surface in a war of words between the two main political parties. On paper, at least, their social and political programmes are similar. It is their followings that make the difference.

Yet the basis of those followings, and their connections to those they follow, have suffered decay. While the parties have strongly-developed cores of adherents, the political base is weak; debates occur, but they do not originate from the rank-and-file members, or from the citizenry at large.

The problem may well go beyond the parties and leaders. One Angolan writer spoke of a general "disenchantment" (*desencanto*) among citizens — disenchantment in regard to power, disenchantment in regard to the image and dream of independence and even disenchantment with opposition voices beyond the two main parties.[1]

Even the opening toward multi-party, western-style democracy, although welcomed, is viewed with some doubt. A leader of a movement among the "third force" groupings, Joaquim Pinto de Andrade, notes the Luanda joke that "there will be no real movement from 'mono-partyism to multi-partyism' but a shift from 'mono to stereo' — the music is the same, but you hear the instruments better."[2] He argues that a representative democracy will not lead to much unless there also comes a "participatory democracy" of collective action among many groupings in civil society.

The scepticism extends beyond the politicians themselves to the new political system which, as yet, shows few signs of delivering the goods. Angolans could find their political aspirations well reflected in the words of Professor Claude Ake, a distinguished Nigerian political scientist:

"The form of democracy demanded is not competitive politics and pluralism and multi-party systems. Rather it is a democracy of concrete rights, particularly economic rights. This democracy is not merely procedural, nor concerned with abstract rights. It has to do with participation.

"This process of participation has been derailed by a whole autocratic elite that inherited the colonial system and did not transform it. Failures of this elite and economic management were so catastrophic that millions of people in Africa are now struggling for mere survival.

"Gaining control is a necessary condition for ordinary people's survival and material benefit, and of course cultural development."[3]

Indeed these words find an echo in an Angolan writer's recent reflections on development in the nation's premier business journal, *Comércio Externo:*

"Political power in this part of the world in most cases finds itself rapidly isolated from the populations who cease to grant it the necessary recognition for it to govern. The non-existence of a real countervailing power has also increased this gap, since the moderating effect that it could exercise ceases to exist, permitting the holders of power to take decisions, often arbitrary, without listening to the opinion of the governed.

"Human needs, self-reliance and organic articulation (between people and nature, civil society and the State, etc.) could be the great pillars so that there is the State and social participation, so that there is participatory dialogue, sustainable development."[4]

The glimpses of Angolans presented in this book in no way contradict these two African observers. War, as it does everywhere, brought out the worst and, sometimes, the best in people.

The best has been worthy of note. To meet their basic needs, Angolans took on most of the burden. If they could hold their ground, literally, they usually succeeded in growing food despite their meagre wherewithal, and despite the probability of pillage.

From the cargo scooters to water-powered grinding mills to windmill pumps — all of them made from wood and other local materials — Angolans showed themselves expert engineers. In keeping 1950s vintage trucks on the roads, they showed themselves expert mechanics.

In their hundreds of thousands of micro-industries, from sandal-making from old tyres, beer-brewing and blacksmithing, Angolans filled gaps that the collapse of industry had widened. In their vigorous networks of trade, often over risky long distances, they kept themselves and others provisioned despite the goods famine. In their stories and riddles and jokes, they kept up their humour and their capacity for social commentary.

In innumerable ways, many of them yet to be identified and acknowledged by outsiders, Angolans survived the war as well as anyone could have. Perhaps better than most; generations of Angolans before them, after all, have known war and how to get through it.

Pointing up the resourcefulness and energy of Angolans could easily lead to myth-making about self-made entrepreneurs and individualists. This is not the intention. Poor Angolans were driven by needs of sheer survival, not self-aggrandizement. As in all Angolan epochs of war, their desperation to survive grew in proportion to the self-aggrandizement of others, whose survival was never in jeopardy.

That struggle for survival had, in itself, destructive consequences. It helped pit Angolan against Angolan, even within clans and families. It tore the social fabric and embedded the practice of solving problems for one's self or a tiny circle regardless of means and regardless of consequences for others. Reinforcing this were the cut-throat norms of an unfettered market, in which few could afford not to participate.

Emotional and social wounds resulting from the war and economic distress may be overcome, but not without some strong acts of will, including a will to put the past behind one, and to get on with one's life. For some, that may take time.

What would quicken the healing?

An apparent and obvious answer could be sought in how Angola's very considerable wealth will be used. Should it be applied to reverse the downward spiral of impoverishment, and therefore to give everyone some confidence about his and her future standard of living, many wounds would no doubt heal.

Another could be what one foreign observer (among several) has noted in Angola: a capacity to forgive. "Wars," wrote Dutch correspondent Koert Lindijer in Angola during one of the deepest points of the war, "especially when ethnic sentiments play a role, show serious excesses, the struggle is bitter. At the end of the day, however....Hate puts down no root."[5]

Even if such an idealization of Angolans is brought down to a more mundane notion that, say, Angolans have a capacity to let bygones be bygones, the essence of that observation provides some grounds for hope.

Finally, there is Angolan nationalism. It is perhaps still an artificial thing, but may be a potential antidote to petty and divisive nationalisms and racism, which are still alive. Angolan social scientists and other observers point out that, compared with the situation in other African countries, most Angolan ethnic groups are embraced wholly within Angolan national territory; their experiences of history have been similar; the war itself — and service in the armed forces in particular — have had homogenizing effects.

On a practical plane, for example, military service spread the use of the Portuguese language in Angola to the point where it can now be termed the language of the nation.

That is, a basis for a national consciousness of *Angolanidade* ("Angolan-ness") has been built to no small degree. On that could be founded social consensus about a project of nation-building. If that holds, then norms of governance which embrace everyone, regardless of background or social standing, may meet no insuperable resistance.

There are some signs, then, that Angolans can build the peace they have wanted for so long. Those powerful interests beyond Angola's borders who had sustained the war have, at last, acceded to that wish. In the balance is the depth of their concern to see all Angolans sustain that peace on terms meaningful to them.

References

Historical Note

1. René Pelissier (1986) <u>História das Campanhas de Angola: Resistência e Revoltas 1845-1941</u>, Volume ii, Imprensa Universitária, Lisboa, page 280. ("O historia da conquista moderna de Angola está regada com o sangue das vitimas.")
2. G. M. Childs (1949) <u>Umbundu Kinship and Character</u>, page 191, cited in Jan Vansina (1966) <u>Kingdoms of the Savanna</u>, University of Wisconsin Press, Madison, page 180.
3. Rene Pelissier (1986) <u>História das Campanhas ...</u>, page 284.
4. Wim Bossema (1988) <u>Angola</u>, Koninklijk, Instituut voor de Tropen, Amsterdam, page 8.
5. Phyllis Johnson & David Martin (1989) <u>Apartheid Terrorism: The Destabilization Report</u>, The Commonwealth Secretariat/James Currey, London, page 123.

Introduction

1. A question posed by British journalist and long-time student of southern African affairs, Joseph Hanlon in his 1991 book <u>Mozambique: Who Calls the Shots?</u>, James Currey, London.
2. Polly Hill (1986) <u>Development Economics on Trial</u>, Cambridge University Press, Cambridge. See especially Chapter 2, "The Vain Search for Universal Generalizations: The Poor Quality of Official Statistics."

Chapter 1

1. Vicki R. Finkel "Red Cross helps population renew life in desolate villages" <u>Southern Africa Online</u> Vol. 4, No. 47 and 48, 1991.
2. E. J. Hobsbawm (1990) <u>Nations and Nationalism Since 1780</u>, Cambridge University Press, Cambridge, page 128.
3. B. E. Harrell-Bond (1986) <u>Imposing Aid: Emergency Assistance to Refugees</u>, Oxford University Press, Oxford, page 7.
4. Irving Kaplan, ed., (1979) <u>Angola: A Country Study</u>, American University, Washington D.C., page 67.
5. Rene Pelissier (1983) "Angola: Physical and Social Geography" <u>Africa South of the Sahara 1983-1984</u>, Europa Publications, London 1983, page 189.
6. Refugee Service, League of Red Cross and Red Crescent Societies, Geneva, typescript dated 30 November 1987.
7. Valerie Curtis (1991) "Angola: The Effects on Women and Children" in Ben Turok, ed., <u>Witness from the Frontline</u>, Institute of African Alternatives, London, page 14.
8. World Bank (1991) <u>Angola: An Introductory Economic Review</u>, Washington D.C., pages 105-106.
9. The other project meriting this adjective was the thrusting tower on Luanda's waterfront, the Neto Mausoleum. "Déficit Orçamental Continua a Crescer", ("Budget Deficit Continues to Grow"), <u>Jornal de Angola</u>, 10 April 1992.
10. International Rescue Committee/S.R. Toussie (1989) "War and Survival in Southern Angola: The Unita Assessment Mission", typescript, page 27.
11. <u>Reisverslag Werkbezoek Angola 21 April-14 Mei 1988</u> (Trip Report Working Visit Angola 21 April-14 May 1988) by Henk van Zuidam, Eduardo Mondlane Stichting, Amsterdam, typescript.
12. UN Special Relief Programme Angola (SRPA) "Situation Report for December 1991", Luanda.
13. <u>Jornal de Angola</u> 2 April and 5 February 1992.
14. UN Special Relief Programme Angola (SRPA) "Situation Report December 1991", Luanda
15. Austin, Ljunggren & Spielberg (23 May 1991) "Needs Assessment: Arriving at a Target Population," Special Relief Programme for Angola (SRPA), typescript, Luanda.
16. Min. do Plano/UNICEF/Oxford Food Studies Group (1991) "Poverty and Food Insecurity in Luanda", Working Paper No. 1, by W. Bender and S. Hunt, Tables 34 and 39. Data from Development Workshop, Luanda, broadly coincide with the Oxford Food Studies/UNICEF survey.

17. HQ UNAVEM II, Verification of Troops in Assembly Areas, March 1992, <u>Jornal de Angola</u>, 27 March 1992.

18. Ministério da Defesa (n.d.) <u>Inquérito Primário: Resultados Preliminares</u>, (Initial Survey: Preliminary Results), typescript, Luanda.

19. L. Rogério "Enfim, um dia tinha que ser!" ("Finally, a day that had to be!") <u>Jornal de Angola</u>, 1 April 1992.

Chapter 2

1. Some questions arise about the gravity of government military injuries in light of data on soldiers discharged as physically unfit. They totalled 29,110, or about half of those wounded on duty. Were many wounds then not serious enough to warrant discharge? It would appear so.

2. David Filipe "Uige: Os Novos Problemas de Caiongo" ("Uige: The New Problems of Caiongo"), <u>Jornal de Angola</u>, 15 January 1992.

3. UN Inter-Agency Task Force (1989) <u>South African Destabilization: The Economic Cost of Frontline Resistance to Apartheid</u>, New York, page 26, citing UNICEF (1987) <u>Children on the Front Line: The impact of apartheid, destabilization and warfare on children in southern and South Africa</u>, (updated in 1989).

4. René Pelissier "Angola: Physical and Social Geography", <u>Africa South of the Sahara 1983-1984</u>, Europa Publications, London, 1983, page 189.

5. Ministry of Health (1990), <u>Relatório da Avaliação das Estratégias de Saúde para todos no Ano 2000</u>, (Evaluation Report of Strategies for Health for all by the year 2000), Luanda, Table 15-E.

6. Ministry of Health (1990) <u>Relatório da Avaliação...</u> (Evaluation Report...), Table 15-F.

7. Unidade Nacional de Alerta Rápido <u>Boletim sobre Segurança Alimentar</u>, (National Early Warning Unit Food Security Bulletin) No. 4/91; and SADCC (1985), <u>Macro-Economic Survey</u>, Table 5, page 168.

8. Dr. David Bernadino (1988) "Contribução para a luta contra a desnutrição: 1. A antropometria nutricional", ("Contribution to the struggle against malnutrition: 1. Nutritional Anthropometry") Instituto Nacional de Saúde Pública, Núcleo Regional do Huambo (National Institute of Public Health, Regional Centre, Huambo) typescript, Luanda. Surveys in Luanda in 1990 showed that a third of all households had at least one child with signs of stunting. See Min. do Plano/UNICEF/Oxford Food Studies Group (1991) "Poverty and Food Insecurity in Luanda" Working Paper No. 1, by W. Bender, S. Hunt, page 34.

9. See data presented in Ministério da Saúde, Programa Nacional de Nutrição <u>Boletim de Vigilância Nutricional</u> (<u>Bulletin of Nutritional Vigilance</u>), No. 1, Setembro 1991.

10. International Rescue Committee/S. R. Toussie (1989) "War and Survival in Southern Angola: The UNITA Assessment Mission", typescript, pages 45-47; and M. N. Vieu, "Kuando Kubango Province: Review of the Nutritional Surveys conducted in Kuando Kubango 1989-1991.", UNICEF, Luanda, typescript.

11. UN Office for Emergencies in Africa, (n.d.) <u>The Emergency Situation in Angola: Priority non-food requirements for the year 1988</u>. Also used for data: UNICEF Area Office Angola <u>Annual Report 1991</u>; UNICEF Area Office Angola <u>Annual Report 1984</u>; Ministério da Saúde, Direcção Nacional de Saúde Pública, <u>Boletim de Vigilância Nutricional</u>, (National Directorate of Public Health, <u>Bulletin of Nutritional Vigilance</u>), Setembro 1991.

12. UNICEF (1992) <u>The State of the World's Children</u>, Oxford University Press, Oxford, Table 2, page 74.

13. Secretariado do Estado de Assuntos Sociais (SEAS) (1991) "Relatório sobre o Projecto de Localização e Colocação Familiar" (State Secretariat for Social Affairs "Report on Tracing and Family Placement Project"), Maria Julia Antonio, Nilsa de Fatima Batalha and Maggie Brown, authors.

14. José Ribeiro "O drama dos filhos da rua" ("The drama of the street children") <u>Jornal de Angola</u>, 12 November 1991, citing an official of SEAS.

15. Manuel Feio "Problemática da crianca de rua foi debatida na UEA" ("Problematic of street children debated at the Union of Angolan Writers"), <u>Jornal de Angola</u>, 6 September 1991.

16. Pereira Santana "Filhos da rua, andarilhos ou futuros delinquentes?" ("Street Children, lay-abouts or future delinquents?"), <u>Jornal de Angola</u>, 23 November 1991

17. Wim Bossema "Angola: Wezen van de Oorlog" ("Angola: Orphans of the War"), <u>Onze Wereld</u> (Amsterdam), March 1989, page 35.

18. N. Boothby, P. Upton, A. Sultan (1991) "Children of Mozambique: The Cost of Survival", typescript, pages 13-17; general impressions gathered at a mid-1991 roundtable of specialists are congruent with the

Mozambican findings. See SEAS (1991) "Mesa Redonda - Educação Para Todos: Apoios ao Desenvolvimento da Educação para Todos, sub-tema 'Educação Para Crianças Vítimas da Guerra'", ("Roundtable - Education for All: Supports to the Development of Education for All, sub-theme 'Education for Child victims of War'") typescript, pages 9-10.

19. "PAZ -- Uma esperança para as mulheres mutiladas" ("Peace -- a Hope for Injured Women"), Jornal de Angola, 28 July 1991.

20. International Rescue Committee/S. R. Toussie (1989) "War and Survival in Southern Angola: the Unita Assessment Mission", pages 31 and 37-38.

21. Renier van de Loo "Angola, Land vol Kalasjnikovws en Kunstbenen" ("Angola: Land full of Kalashnikovs and Artificial Limbs"), Utrechts Nieuwsblad, Utrecht, The Netherlands, 6 June 1987.

22. Anne Beamish and Will Donovan (1987) "Vocational Workshops Programme for the Civilian War Disabled and Physically Handicapped in Angola", report for Development Workshop, Luanda.

23. Mutilados matam comandante das TGFA do Cunene" (War-injured kill commander of the Border Troops of Cunene"), Jornal de Angola, 25 September 1991.

Chapter 3

1. Up to the early 1980s, an estimated 5,000 to 10,000 skilled Angolans left the country for Portugal and Brazil. More followed through the balance of the 1980s. See M. R. Bhagavan "Angola: Survival Strategies for a Socialist State", Economic and Political Weekly, New Delhi, 6 August 1988, page 1635.

2. About 55 percent of all Angolans alive in 1992 were born after 1971.

3. Ministério da Agricultura (1991) Agropecuária em Cifras, (Agriculture and Livestock in Figures), Tables 29, 12; World Bank (1991) Angola: An Introductory Economic Review, page 250.

4. Drawn from, inter alia, personal communications with Angolan rural development specialists Fernando Pacheco dos Santos and Vítor Serrano; Senior Agronomist Erwin Konig of ICRC, and Oxfam (UK) Representative in Angola, Andrew Couldridge.

5. Júlio de Morais (1991) Fernando Pacheco Diagnóstico das Associações de Camponeses em Angola, (Assessment of Peasant Associations in Angola), ADRA/ACORD, page 66.

6. Even where provincial conditions for delivery of relief were good, such as in Huila which suffered the fewest problems of accessibility in the 1980s, the degree of dependence on relief food was very modest indeed. See De Morais and Pacheco, p. 62. A study of food aid via a large church charity using European foodstuffs in the 1980s revealed that foodstuffs distributed in rural areas could only rarely have fed a person for more than two weeks' in any given year -- and that for only tiny fractions of the total population.

   However, for known and specified populations (such as those serviced by the ICRC in Huambo, Bie and Benguela) the contribution was more vital, but again not crucial to survival.

   The point is that for the overwhelming majority in Angola's rural areas, food aid was just one among several sources of food.

7. Jan Vansina (1966) The Kingdoms of the Savanna, The University of Wisconsin Press, Madison, page 200.

8. Agnes Morel (1990) "Formação para o Trabalho no Sector 'Informal'," ("Training for Work in the 'Informal' Sector"), typescript, International Labour Organization, Luanda.

9. Food and Agriculture Organization (1984) SADCC Agriculture: Toward 2000, Table 4.1.

10. Agnes Morel (1990) "Formação para o Trabalho no Sector 'Informal'," typescript, ILO, Table 1, page 7.

11. "Angola: War, Disease Grips Siego City", Southern Africa Chronicle, 12 February 1990.

12. Vítor Serrano and Richard C. Carter (1991) "Small Scale Irrigation in Angola: Potential and Promise", Outlook on Agriculture, Vol. 20 No. 3, pp 175-181.

13. CARE International (1990) Needs Assessment Survey: Cunene Province. The essential message of this report was to caution both donors and administrators against an ill-considered rush to provide food aid when, for the broad population, none was needed.

14. "A Lenha e o Carvão Vegetal na RPA" ("Firewood and Charcoal in the People's Republic of Angola") (1989), O Renovável Ano 2 No. 6, page 9.

15. ETC Foundation (1987) "SADCC Energy Development: Fuelwood; Report on Angola", typescript.

16. Ministério do Plano, INE, (1990) "Famílias e Aldeias do Sul de Angola: Análise dum Inquérito Sócio-Económico-Demográfico nas Zonas Rurais da Região Sul-Sudoeste" ("Families and villages in the south of Angola: Analysis of a socio-economic-demographic survey in the rural zones of the south-southwest region"), typescript, Luanda.

17. UNDP/OPE ANG-84/009 (1989) <u>Reconstruction Programme for the Provinces of Huila, Namibe and Cunene, Phase II, Vol. 6: Project Profiles</u>, page 110.

18. E. Frigyes and J. M. V. Bessa (1989) "O Mercado Paralelo de Luanda", ("The Parallel Market of Luanda"), typescript, Luanda, page 17.

19. Ministério do Plano/UNICEF/Food Studies Group Oxford (1991) "Short and Medium Term Options for the Alleviation of Poverty in Luanda" by William Bender and Simon Hunt, Luanda Household Budget and Nutrition Survey, Working Paper No. 2, page 20.

20. This is a major theme of such recent books as <u>From Feast to Famine: Official Cures and Grassroots Remedies to Africa's Crisis</u> by Bill Rau, Zed Books, London, 1991 and <u>Listening to Africa: Developing Africa from the Grassroots</u>, by Pierre Pradervand, Praeger, New York, 1990.

Chapter 4

1. Economist Intelligence Unit (EIU)/Hodges (1987) <u>Angola to the 1990s: The Potential for Recovery, Special Report No. 1079</u>, page 85. Data on landholdings refers to 1970. I. Kaplan, ed. (1979) <u>Angola: A Country Study</u>, Washington D.C., page 208, reports Food and Agriculture Organization (FAO) estimate of only 1.8 million hectares actually in use in 1975. Rangelands used by semi-nomadic pastoralists, perhaps covering 29 million hectares, are not included in these figures.

2. Ministério da Agricultura e Desenvolvimento Rural, Dept de Estatística (1991) <u>Agropecária de Angola em Cifras</u> (Angolan Agriculture and Livestock in Figures), Tabela 11, plus authors' calculations based on output figures presented in Tabela 3.

3. World Bank (1991) <u>Angola: An Introductory Economic Review</u>, page 245.

4. World Bank (1991) <u>Angola: An Introductory Economic Review</u>.

5. David Filipe, "Os Novos Problemas de Caiongo" ("The New Problems of Caiongo"), <u>Jornal de Angola</u>, 15 January, 1992; "Estradas Intrasitáveis Prejudicam programa do Governo", ("Impassable Roads Hurt Government Programme"), <u>Jornal de Angola</u>, 12 March, 1992.

6. Irving Kaplan, ed. (1979) <u>Angola: A Country Study</u>, American University, Washington D.C., page 238.

7. Economist Intelligence Unit/Hodges (1987) <u>Angola to the 1990s</u>, page 111.

8. Diogo Paixão "Estradas e Pontes: Onde Tudo Começa e Acaba" ("Roads and Bridges: Where Everything Begins and Ends"), <u>Jornal de Angola</u>, 6 November, 1991.

9. UNDP/OPE - Ministry of Planning, <u>Reconstruction Programme for the Provinces of Huila, Namibe and Cunene Phase II Volume 2: Sectoral Studies 2b Infrastructure</u>, page 45.

10. World Bank (1991) <u>Angola: An Introductory Economic Review</u>, page 262, citing 1986 government data. René Pelissier (1983) "Angola: Economy" in <u>Africa South of the Sahara 1983-1984</u>, Europa Publications, London, page 198.

11. World Bank (1991) <u>Angola: An Introductory Economic Review</u>, pages 262-263.

12. "Reabertas Carreiras da EVA" ("EVA Routes Re-opened"), <u>Jornal de Angola</u>, 19 January, 1992.

13. "Fabimor lança motociclos indianos" ("Fabimor launches Indian motorcycles"), <u>Jornal de Angola</u>, 10 November, 1992; "Fabimor: bicicletas já rolam" ("Fabimor: Bicycles Already Rolling"), <u>Jornal de Angola</u>, 14 February, 1992.

14. "Comboio vai a Malanje custe o que custar" ("The train is going to Malanje no matter what"), <u>Jornal de Angola</u>, 6 August, 1991.

15. Benguela Railways, <u>Editorial Vanguarda</u>, cited in Phyllis Johnson & David Martin (1989) <u>Apartheid Terrorism: The Destabilization Report</u>, The Commonwealth Secretariat/James Currey, London, pages 130-131.
Worker deaths: "Uncertain Future for War-Damaged Benguela Line", <u>The Herald</u> (Harare), 22 August, 1991, page 10.

16. World Bank (1991) <u>Angola: An Introductory Economic Review</u>, Table VIII.6, page 266.

17. Luanda-Malanje source: interview with CFL director Antonio Agante, "CFL sempre foram tratados como enteado" ("Luanda Railways always treated as a step-child"), <u>Jornal de Angola</u>, 3 September, 1991.
Lobito Corridor: Mario Paiva, "Window on the Atlantic for Southern Africa", <u>SADCC Energy</u>, Luanda No.1, 1988, page 4.
Namibe-Jamba: UNDP/OPE - Ministry of Planning, <u>Reconstruction Programme for the Provinces of Huila, Namibe and Cunene, Phase II Volume 6 Project Profiles</u>.

18. "CFB já reparou 300 quilómetros de via" ("Benguela Railways already repaired 300 kilometres of route"), Jornal de Angola, 3 August, 1991.

19. World Bank (1991) Angola: An Introductory Economic Review, citing 1987 government sources, page 285; Diogo Paixão, "Prejuízos provocados pela guerra elevam-se a 22 milhões de dólares", ("War losses rise to 22 million dollars"), Jornal de Angola, 15 August, 1991.

20. EIU/Hodges (1987) Angola to the 1990s.

21. "Project G-E-1 Repair and Extension of Lomaum Hydroelectric Power Plant" SADCC Energy No. 1, Luanda, 1988, page 5.

22. Jornal de Angola, 24 November 1991.

23. The most complete record of oil industry damage to 1989 is that contained in Apartheid Terrorism: The Destabilization Report, Phyllis Johnson & David Martin (1989), The Commonwealth Secretariat/James Currey, London, pages 128-129.

24. Adão Faustino, "'JA' na Lunda-Sul(2): Saúde e Educação, um mar de problemas", ("'Jornal de Angola' in Lunda-sul(2): Health and Education, A sea of problems"), Jornal de Angola, 6 February, 1992.

25. "Vila de Bocoio tem de ser completamente reconstruída", ("Town of Bocoio has to be completely reconstructed"), Jornal de Angola, 9 August, 1991.

26. "Jorge Valentim (UNITA): Ajuda americana visa fins humanitarios" ("Jorge Valentim (UNITA): American aid has humanitarian aims") Jornal de Angola, 3 December, 1991. Earlier UNITA claims were somewhat different, so it is not clear just how many actually existed at any given time.

    "Statistics given by UNITA officials... and in a report from the UNITA Secretariat for Education and Culture claimed over 200,000 students in UNITA schools, over 2,000 of them secondary students (5th grade and up). The figures given showed dramatic shifts from year-to-year. In 1986, for example, [Jonas] Savimbi said UNITA had 6,951 primary schools; a table in UNITA's own education report said there were 976 primary schools in 1987 and 3,139 in 1988. The number of primary teachers went from 7,127 in 1986...to 3,003 in 1987 and 8,611 in 1988 according to the education report. The data provided by the interviewees makes the largest of these numbers unlikely, but provides no basis for an alternative numerical estimate."

    William Minter (1990) "The National Union for the Total Independence of Angola (UNITA) as Described by Ex-participants and Foreign Visitors" (later published by AEI/AWEPAA) paper, Washington D. C., p. 11.

27. Estimates of current replacement costs.

    Rural Primary school, equipped: US$4,500 per classroom

    Urban primary school, equipped: US$9,000 per classroom

    Secondary school, equipped: US$10,000 per classroom.

    Assuming that 70 percent of the estimated 11,000 lost classrooms were rural primary, 10 percent urban primary and 20 percent secondary, we arrive at the following calculations:

    7,700 x $4,500 = US$34.7 million

    1,100 x $9,000 = US$9.9 million

    2,200 x $10,000 = US$22 million

    Total: US$66.6 million

    The province of Benguela estimates the cost of rehabilitating 61 schools at 1.5 billion New Kwanzas, or US$2.7 million at the rate of exchange 550 Nkw = US $1. Assuming that schools have six classrooms (some more, many less) the calculations just made appear reasonable.

28. "Salas/Contentores no Internato '1 de Junho'" ("Container-Classrooms in the '1st of June boarding school'"), Jornal de Angola, 8 February 1992, describing two ocean-going containers at a Catholic centre in Luanda, remodelled as classrooms serving 36 students per shift.

29. Data on Malanje from: Valerie Curtis (1991) "Angola: Effects on Women and Children" in Ben Turok, ed., Witness from the Frontline, Institute for African Alternatives, London, page 14; national data from: United Nations Office for Emergencies in Africa (1988) The Emergency Situation in Angola, page 51.

30. Ministério da Saúde, Gabinete do Plano (1991) Relatório do Plano de Recuperação Económica 1990 (Report of the Economic Reconstruction Plan 1990), Luanda, Tables 18 and 14.

31. UNITA information attached to UNICEF Emergency (1991) "Cuando Cuabango Province, Project Health Sector", Luanda.

32. International Rescue Committee/S. R. Toussie (1989) "War and Survival in Southern Angola: The UNITA Mission".

33. UNICEF Luanda Office (1992) <u>Angola Basic Data</u>, and International Rescue Committee/S. R. Toussie (1989) "War and Survival in Southern Angola", pages 36-37 and 42, which suggests that, as of late 1989, UNITA vaccination efforts had failed due to lack of training.

34. T. Cohen, M. O. Santos Ferreira, S. Chamaret and Luc Montagnier, <u>Journal of Acquired Immune Deficiency Syndromes</u>, Vol. 3, No. 8, 1990, reported in Messias Constantino, "A doenca do século está entre nós", ("The Disease of the Century is in our midst"), <u>Jornal de Angola</u>, 8 December, 1991.

35. Government of the R. P. de Angola/João Seródio de Almeida (1991) "Relatório Nacional à Conferência das Nações Unidas para o Ambiente e Desenvolvimento, Brasil 1992", ("National Report to the Conference of the United Nations for the Environment, Brazil 1992"), page 29.

36. Valerie Curtis (1991) "Angola: Effects on Women and Children" in Ben Turok, ed., <u>Witness from the Frontline</u>, Institute for African Alternatives, London, page 16.

37. "Instituto de Investigação Reabilita Estações Experimentais Agrícolas", ("Research Institute Repairing Agricultural Research Stations"), <u>Jornal de Angola</u>, 12 March, 1992.

38. "Reabilitação de Infrastruturas No Zaire" ("Repair of Infrastructures in Zaire Province"), <u>Jornal de Angola</u>, 3 February, 1992.

39. "No Bié: Reabilitação de Infrastruturas orça em cerca de 7 milhoes de Nkz" ("In Bié: Repair of infrastructures budgetted at about 7 million new kwanzas"), <u>Jornal de Angola</u>, 25 February, 1992.

40. Ministério do Plano/UNICEF/Oxford Food Studies Group (1991) "Strategic Options for Health Service Provision in Luanda", The Luanda Household Budget and Nutrition Survey, Working Paper No. 5, by Stephen Devereux and Simon Hunt, page 16 and passim.

41. Phyllis Johnson & David Martin (1989) <u>Apartheid Terrorism: The Destabilization Report,</u> The Commonwealth Secretariat, James Currey, London, page 123.

Chapter 5

1. Government of the R. P. de Angola (1982) <u>Livro Branco das Agressões do Regime Racista da Africa do Sul contra a Republica Popular de Angola</u>, (White Book of the Aggressions of the Racist Regime of South Africa Against the People's Republic of Angola), Luanda, page 64.

2. Angolan estimate, presented to United Nations Security Council, S/17648, 22 November 1985.

3. UNICEF (1987) <u>Children on the Frontline</u>, page 34.

4. UN Inter-Agency Task Force (1989) <u>South African Desabilization: The Economic Cost of Frontline Resistance to Apartheid</u>, New York, page 6.

5. Phyllis Johnson & David Martin (1989) <u>Apartheid Terrorism: The Destabilization Report</u>, Commonwealth Secretariat/James Currey, London, pages 122-149.

6. Angolan Official estimate, 1991, reported in various news agency accounts, e.g. <u>Business Day</u> (Johannesburg), 11 June, 1991.

7. Economist Intelligence Unit/Hodges (1987), <u>Angola to the 1990s</u>, page 35.

8. <u>Southscan</u>, 5 July, 1991.

9. "Juntas e dólares" ("Limbs and Dollars"), <u>Jornal de Angola</u>, 13 March, 1992.

10. See, for example, Henrique Guerra (1979) <u>Angola: Estrutura Económica e Classes Sociais</u> (Angola: Economic Structure and Social Classes); World Bank (1991) <u>Angola: An Introductory Economic Review</u>; and R. Aguilar and Mário Zejan (1991) <u>Angola 1991: A Long Hard Way to the Marketplace</u>, Dept. of Economics, University of Gothenburg.

11. World Bank (1991) <u>Angola: An Introductory Economic Review</u>, page 193.

12. For a view of deterioration in one of Angola's rural heartlands, already well advanced in the later years of colonial rule, see: Hermann Possinger (1973) "Interrelations between Economic and Social Change in Rural Africa: The Case of the Ovimbundu of Angola" in F-W. Heimer, ed., <u>Social Change in Angola</u>, Weltforum Verlag, Munich, pages 31-52.

13. Ervin Frigyes, Júlio M.V. Bessa (1989) "O Mercado Parallelo de Luanda", ("The Parallel Market of Luanda") Luanda, typescript, page 17.

14. "Muck and Brass" <u>Market Southeast</u>, 4 December 1989. In Nigeria, the rates are said to be between 10 and 20 percent. See Michelle Faul, "Nigerians Describe Land of Corruption" (Associated Press feature) in <u>The Herald</u> (Harare) 7 May, 1992.

15. Richard Gerster, (1989) "How to Ruin a Country: The Case of Togo" <u>IFDA Dossier</u>, No. 71, pages 26-36, and a 1990 World Bank study by Alexander Yeats, reported in <u>The Herald</u> (Harare), 14 June, 1990 "Africa ripped off on trade".

16. Osvaldo Van-Dunem, Governor of Huambo Province, cited in Eugenio Diogo "Huambo Um amanhã diferente" ("Huambo: A Different Tomorrow") <u>Comércio Externo</u>, September 1991, page 30.

Chapter 6

1. Africa Watch (1991) <u>Angola: Civilians Devastated by 15 Year War</u>, page 2, cites unnamed sources estimating 60,000 anti-personnel mines. <u>SouthScan</u>, 9 August, 1991 cites unnamed officials estimating one million mines.

2. <u>Jornal de Angola</u>, 28 July, 1991; 7 April, 1992.

3. United Nations "Situation Report 01/92 on Emergency Relief operations in Angola 01-31 January 1992", page 7.

4. <u>Jornal de Angola</u>, 10 November, 1991.

5. Rae McGrath (1990) "Mine Warfare: an Aid Issue", <u>Refugees Participation Network</u> No. 9, pages 3-6.

6. "Especialistas das FAA exibem nova tecnologia de desminagem" ("Specialists of the Angolan Armed Forces show new de-mining technology") <u>Jornal de Angola</u>, 3 April, 1992.

7. The 1988 figure is from: Ministério da Saúde (1990) <u>Relatório da Avaliação das Estratégias de Saúde para Todos no Ano 2000</u>, (Evaluation Report of Strategies for Health for All by 2000), page 70, citing Ministério do Trabalho e Segurança Social (Ministry of Labour and Social Security); the estimate for 1992 of 70,000 is from the United Church of Canada, Toronto, <u>Angola</u> (pamphlet).

8. Neto Makandumba, "Minas continuam a fazer vitimas" ("Mines continue to claim victims"), <u>Jornal de Angola</u>, 27 March, 1992.

9. Carlos Miranda, "Gigantes metálicos rodeados por trepadeiras e muitas minas" ("Metal giants surrounded by vines and many mines"), <u>Jornal de Angola</u>, 8 December 1991.

10. Cesar Andre "Elefantes abatidos com minas anti-tanque" ("Elephants cut down by anti-tank mines"), <u>Jornal de Angola</u>, 27 December 1991.

11. "Extensão da administração em Malanje" ("Extension of Administration in Malanje"), <u>Jornal de Angola</u>. 15 March 1992.

12. "Governo 'travado' em Monte Belo" ("Government 'braked' in Monte Belo"), <u>Jornal de Angola</u>, 5 December 1991.

13. "Adeptos do MPLA e da UNITA envolvidos em escaramuças" ("Followers of MPLA and UNITA involved in skirmishes"), <u>Jornal de Angola</u>, 31 January 1992; "Governo e UNITA recolhem armas" ("Government and UNITA collect arms"), <u>Jornal de Angola</u>, 19 February 1992.

14. "A rua pertence aos corajosos" ("The street belongs to the brave"), <u>Jornal de Angola 28</u>, September 1991.

15. David Filipe, "Uige: Paz, para que te quero?!" ("Uige: Peace, why should I love you?!"), <u>Jornal de Angola</u>, 31 January 1992.

16. Jaime Azulay, "Canjala: Assaltos na estrada" ("Canjala: Attacks on the highway"), <u>Correio da Semana</u>, 17 February 1992.

17. "Paiol da UNITA descoberto na Kibala" ("UNITA cache found at Kibala"), <u>Jornal de Angola</u>, 21 February 1992.

18. "Policia adoptará nova estratégia" ("Police will adopt a new strategy"), <u>Jornal de Angola</u>, 8 January 1992.

19. "Policia quer 'travar' carbonização de ladroes" ("Police want to put a brake on the burning of thieves"), <u>Jornal de Angola</u>, 21 December, 1991.

20. Agostinho Tchitata "A deliquência anda a solta nos bairros da capital" ("Delinquency running loose in neighbourhoods of the capital"), <u>Jornal de Angola</u>, 5 February, 1992.

Chapter 7

1. As the Catholic Institute for International Relations (CIIR) points out in a recent booklet, Catholicism was the colonial orthodoxy. Relations between the Roman Catholic Church and Portugal (and hence, Angola as a province of Portugal) were governed by a concordat -- an international agreement between the Pope and a secular government -- making the Church an official state institution with delineated roles and rights, something other churches did not have. With the abrogation of the concordat after Angolan independence,

church-state relations worsened. Meanwhile, "the Protestant Angolan Council of Churches has actively supported the liberation struggle in Namibia and the democratic movement in South Africa". CIIR (1991) Angola: The Possible Peace, London, page 13.

2. Radio report, Radio Nacional de Angola, Luanda, 17.7.91, 19:00 gmt.

3. "Angola: Religious Riot", Africa Confidential, 4 March 1987; "Opposition Groups" West Africa, 2 March 1987; "L'Unita soutient la secte tocoiste" Marches Tropicaux, 6 March 1987.

4. MPLA-Partido do Trabalho (1990) "Resolução Especial Sobre o Multipartidarismo", III Congresso" , part III No. 2.

5. However, only 26 were able to send delegates to the Multiparty Conference of January 1992. And by mid-April 1992 only four new parties had met the (by then lowered) minimum requirements for official recognition as political parties. The PRD and FDA had met the requirement of collecting 3,000 signatures gathered from residents of at least 14 of Angola's 18 provinces, as stipulated under law 15/91; the new law, under which PAJOCA and PSD gained official status, lowered the requirement to 1,500 signatures of residents of at least 10 provinces. "Angola: The Multi-Party Takeover", Africa Confidential, 30 August 1991; "Nova lei dos partidos politicos 'promove' PAJOCA, FDA e PSD" (New Lease on Political Parties "Promotes' PAJOCA, FDA AND PSD"), Jornal de Angola, 10 April 1992.

6. "Comércio Livre Foi Retomado no Bié" (Free Trade Resumes in Bié"), Jornal de Angola, 15 August, 1992.

7. See Rev. Ben Chavis (1988) "Report on the Visit of African-American Church and Community Leaders to the People's Republic of Angola", United Church of Christ, USA. Reports a number of war deaths among Angolan Protestant leaders.

8. Radek Sikorski (1989) "The Mystique of Savimbi", National Review, 18 August, pp 34-37; this magazine is a publication of the right wing in the US; various statements by Paulino Pinto João, President of the National Democratic Convention of Angola (CNDA) and former Director, MPLA Department of Information and Propaganda.

9. João Melo, "Comentarios as mudancas constitucionais propostas pelo Governo angolano" ("Commentaries on the constitutional changes proposed by the Angolan government"), Jornal de Angola, 16 January, 1992.

10. "Cenário social, religioso, e cultural da situação political angolana" ("Social, religious, and cultural panoramo of the Angolan political situation") report on a colloquium among six Angolan intellectuals held at CIDAC in Lisbon in late 1991, reported in Correio da Semana, 4 May, 1992; see especially page 16 for observations on the gap in public discourse between political elite and citizenry.

11. Jonuel Goncalves "A difícil emergência da sociedade civil" ("The difficult emergence of civil society"), Correio da Semana, 6 April, 1992.

12. The term "fragilizada" is that of Angolan sociologist Ana Maria de Oliveira; interview, Luanda, December 1991.

13. See "Cenário social, religioso e cultural da situação politica angolana", Correio da Semana, 4 May, 1992.

14. Domingos Jacinto "Juventude: Um modo de viver e de actuar" ("Youth: A way of living and acting"), Jornal de Angola, 12 December, 1991.

15. Sousa Jamba (1990) Patriots, Penguin, London page 15.

16. Jornal de Angola, 13 August, 1991; 13 September, 1991; and 28 September, 1991; personal communication from Allan Cain, Development Workshop, Luanda.

17. UNICEF (1992) State of the World's Children 1992, Tables 5 and 9; and RPA, Ministério da Saúde (1991) Relatório Estatístico de 1989 ("1989 Statistical Report"), which shows a rate of material mortality in hospitals in 1989 of 665 per 100,000 pregnancies handled (Table 5.8 p 50). The average rate for UNICEF's 39 countries in the "very high under-five mortality rate" category is 570 per 100,000 pregnancies.

18. UNICEF (1992) State of the World's Children 1992, page 78.

19. Wim Bossema "Angolese kerken zijn de snelst groeiende in Afrika" ("Angolan churches are the fastest-growing in Africa"), De Volkskrant (Amsterdam), 21 June, 1988.

20. "Lisboa Santos ao 'JA': 'Igreja pode influenciar moralização da sociedade'" ("Lisboa Santos to the Jornal de Angola: The church can influence the moral uplift of society"), Jornal de Angola, 5 April 1992.

21. "Que Haja Paz" ("Let there be peace"), Comércio Externo, June 1991, page 5.

Chapter 8

1. As reported by David Gallagher of Oxfam-Canada.

2.   UNICEF (1992) <u>The State of the World's Children 1992</u>, Table 1. On the table of basic indicators, the most important is the annual number of deaths of children under five years of age. Countries are ranked according to that indicator, as the most sensitive measurement available of overall well-being.

3.   Population Crisis Committee 1987. The index combines general life expectancy and other common measures of living standards.

4.   UNDP (1991) <u>Human Development Report 1991</u>, New York.

5.   Ken Post and Phil Wright (1989) <u>Socialism and Under Development</u>, Routledge, London, Chapter Three.

6.   Gerald J. Bender (1978) <u>Angola Under the Portuguese</u>, pages 229-30, states that only about half of all settlers could read and write. The World Bank states that "over half of the.. white settlers had never gone to school and the vast majority had less than four years of education." World Bank (1991) <u>Angola: An Introductory Economic Review</u>, page 175. The point is disputed by some Angolans, however.

7.   World Bank (1991) <u>Angola: An Introductory Economic Review</u>, page 186.

8.   Neto Makandumba "Kwanza-Sul: Vencer o atraso económico provocado pela guerra" ("Kwanza-Sul: Overcoming the economic delay provoked by war"), <u>Jornal de Angola</u>, 20 September, 1991.

9.   World Bank (1991) <u>Angola: An Introductory Economic Review</u>, page 41.

10.   World Bank (1990) <u>Development Report 1990</u>, Washington, DC.

11.   A researcher specializing in the peasant question in Angola, cited in Pierre Beaudet et al. (1991) <u>Angola 1991: un pays a refaire</u>, Montreal, page 38.

12.   <u>Jornal de Angola</u>, 7 February, 1992.

13.   This section draws heavily on Júlio de Morais and Fernando Pacheco (1991) "Diagóstico das Associações de Camponeses em Angola", and F. Pacheco (1991) "Rural Development in Angola: The State and the ONGs," speech delivered to the international seminar on NGOs in Angola, Amsterdam, 15 June, 1991.

14.   World Bank (1991) <u>Angola: An Introductory Economic Review</u>, page 35.

15.   "Angola: Living with War", <u>Africa Confidential</u>, 13 May, 1987, page 5.

16.   Anita Coulson "Angola's Change of Clothes" <u>Southern African Economist</u>, October/November 1990, page 37; and "Angola adopts steps to cut debt", <u>The Herald</u> (Harare) 21 September, 1990.

17.   Ministério do Plano/UNICEF/Oxford Food Studies Group (1992) "Poverty and Food Insecurity in Luanda", The Luanda Household Budget and Nutrition Survey, Working Paper No. 1, by W. Bender and S. Hunt, page 47. The paper defines the poverty line as a level of household income equal to two-thirds the median level of household income in Luanda in early 1990. That median was about US$25-a-month at parallel market rates of exchange, and about US$1,700-a-month at official exchange rates.

18.   Ministério do Plano/UNICEF/Oxford Food Studies Group (1992) "Short and Medium Term Options for the Alleviation of Poverty in Luanda", Luanda Household Budget and Nutritional Survey Working Paper No. 2, by W. Bender and S. Hunt, page 9.

19.   "$2.2bn in oil revenues", <u>Southscan</u>, 21 February, 1992.

20.   A gesture which won a banner headline -- "IMF GENEROUS" -- in Luanda's daily newspaper, <u>Jornal de Angola</u>, 9 April, 1992. In May 1992 the World Bank began disbursing US$95 million in loans for three projects: training technocrats in economic management; hiring consulting services to make a blueprint for infrastructure rehabilitation; and upgrading of water and sanitation for the cities of Lobito and Benguela.

21.   The mediocre, if not negative results of structural adjustment programmes have been reviewed succinctly in Roger C. Riddell, "Losing the 90s. Another declining decade for African development", CIIR briefing Paper, London, May 1992. Riddell cites numerous studies, including those by the World Bank and IMF themselves, on this poor performance of structural adjustment programmes.

22.   Ministério do Plano/UNICEF/Oxford Food Studies Group (1992) "Poverty and Food Insecurity in Luanda", The Luanda Household Budget and Nutrition Survey, Working Paper No. 1, by W. Bender and S. Hunt, page 1. They base these conclusions on work done by other economists, and cite in particular the work of the distinguished British economist Frances Stewart, who has, with others, monitored the impact of structural adjustment programmes in Africa since the early 1980s. For the broader framework, see: A. MacEwan and W. K. Tabb, eds., (1989) <u>Instability and Change in the World Economy</u>, Monthly Review Press, New York, especially R. E. Wood, "The International Monetary Fund and the World Bank in a Changing World Economy", pages 298-315.

23.   Giovanni Andrea Cornia (1987) "Adjustment Policies 1980-1985: Effects on Child Welfare" in Cornia, Jolly and Stewart, eds., <u>Adjustment with a Human Face: Protecting the Vulnerable and Promoting Growth</u>, Volume I, Oxford University Press, Oxford, page 66.

24. Salim Lone "Adjustment Programmes under fire: Human dimension is neglected, asserts Khartoum declaration", <u>Africa Recovery</u>, June 1988.

25. Attributed to US political activist, Jesse Jackson, cited in Carol B. Thompson (1991) <u>Harvests Under Fire: Regional Co-operation for Food Security in Southern Africa</u>, Zed Books, London, page 108.

26. <u>Update Angola</u>, December 1991, United Church of Canada, Toronto, page 5.

Chapter 9

1. Jofere Justino (of the UNITA newspaper) quoted in "Cenário social, religioso e cultural da situação política angolana" ("Social, religious and cultural panorama of the Angolan political situation"), report of a discussion at CIDAC in Lisbon in late 1991, <u>Correio da Semana</u>, 4 May, 1992.

2. Fernando Dacosta "Soares e Pinto de Andrade num colóquio sobre Africa: Cooperação não pode ser caridade nem negócio" ("Soares and Pinto de Andrade in a colloquium on Africa: Cooperation can be neither charity nor business"), <u>Público</u> (Lisbon), 25 May 1991 ("Do monopartidarismo para o multi-partidarismo, mais uma passagem 'de mono para o estéreo', a música é a mesma, os instrumentos é que se ouvem melhor").

3. Interview by Glenda Daniels "Africa's second independence", <u>Work in Progress</u>, (Johannesburg) January/February 1992, page 44.

4. João Rodrigues "Deus não faz morada" ("God makes no home"), <u>Comércio</u> Externo, June, 1991, pages 69, 71

5. Koert Lindijer "Haat Schiet Geen Wortel" ("Hate Puts Down No Root"), De Volkskrant (Amsterdam), 8 July, 1991.

Further Readings

Africa Watch (1991) <u>Angola: Civilians Devastated by 15 Year War</u>, Washington D. C.

Pierre Beaudet, et al (1991) <u>Angola 1991. Un Pays a Refaire</u>, Montreal, Canada.

G. J. Bender (1978) <u>Angola under the Portuguese. The Myth and the Reality</u>, London.

M. R. Bhagavan (1986) <u>Angola's Political Economy 1975-1985</u>, Uppsala, Sweden.

Fred Bridgland (1986) <u>Jonas Savimbi: A Key to Africa</u>, London.

Horace Campbell (1990) <u>The Siege of Cuito Cuanavale</u>, Uppsala, Sweden.

Joseph Hanlon (1986) <u>Beggar Your Neighbours: Apartheid Power in Southern Africa</u>, London.

H. Hansen, R. Hansen, E. K. Johansson (1989) <u>Women of Angola</u>, Bergen, Norway.

Sousa Jamba (1990) <u>Patriots</u>, London.

Phyllis Johnson & David Martin (1989) <u>Apartheid Terrorism. The Destabilization Report</u>, London.

Phyllis Johnson & David Martin (1988) <u>Front Line Southern Africa: Destructive Engagement</u>, New York.

R. Kapuscinski (1987) <u>Another Day of Life</u>, London.

William Minter (1990) <u>Account from Angola. UNITA as described by ex-participants and foreign visitors</u>, Amsterdam/Uppsala.

William Minter (1988) <u>Operation Timber</u>, New York.

Pepetela (1983) <u>Mayombe</u>, Harare/London.

John Stockwell (1978) <u>In Search of Enemies: A CIA Story</u>, New York.

Finn Tarp (1992) <u>Angola. Background Report and Possibilities for Danish Development Assistance</u>, Danida, Copenhagen.

Graham Walker (1990) <u>Angola: The Promise of Riches</u>, London.